ESCAPE TO LIVE

ESCAPE TO LIVE

by

WING COMMANDER

EDWARD HOWELL

OBE, DFC

GROSVENOR

LONDON · MELBOURNE · WELLINGTON

GROSVENOR BOOKS
54 LYFORD ROAD, LONDON SW18 3JJ
21 DORCAS STREET, S. MELBOURNE, VICTORIA 3205, AUSTRALIA
P O BOX 1834, WELLINGTON, NEW ZEALAND

First published in 1947 by Longmans, Green & Co Ltd, London
This edition published 1981
Reprinted 1984
Cover design by Cameron Johnson

PRINTED BY COLORCRAFT LTD, HONG KONG

To
all those who have
sacrificed that we might Escape to Live.
In gratitude to my Parents and
to the People of Greece
and to
The host of comrades in the Royal Air Force
who have given their lives
and to
Frank and another host who give everything.

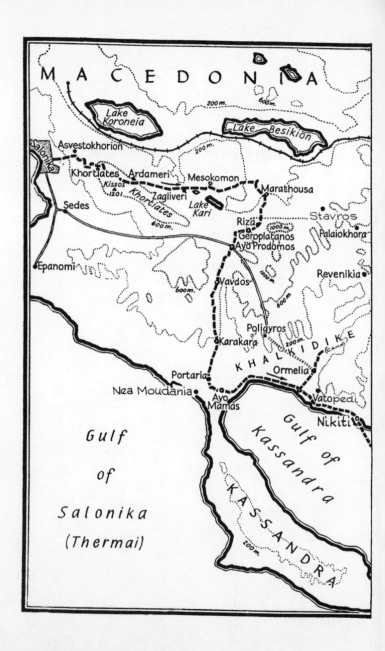

In the blue Cretan sky a lone flier fighting,
   The last upholder of the free,
Falls, and an unseen finger writing,
   Marks, marks him for liberty.

Past the dim edge of serfdom and of dying
   An imperious whisper led
Through suffering, danger — star its light supplying —
   Home, home from the dead.

Who have escaped to live, immortal band,
   Set now your nations free,
Take God's great sword of freedom in your hand
   And strike, strike for Liberty.

MORRIS MARTIN

CONTENTS

I

CRETE — PRELUDE

I

It was cold in the early morning as the first glimmer of light announced another day. The world seemed to be wondering whether it was worth waking up at all; the birds and the trees and even the mountains seemed to be holding their breath, listening. Only the whisper of the ripples on the nearby beach broke the stillness.

But if you held your breath and listened too, you could hear other sounds. Men were moving about in the distance, their footsteps and voices muffled as if by the darkness. I moved away from my tent in the olive grove, down the hillside and on to the road that flanked the landing strip. At the end of the strip three Hurricane single-seater fighters were lined up, ready to take off at a moment's notice; one of them was mine.

The strip was Maleme airfield in Crete and it was the 14th of May 1941.

I clambered awkwardly into the unfamiliar cockpit. I had never flown a Hurricane before, but I did not want anyone to know that. I had managed to conceal the fact from the Commander-in-Chief when he had given me the squadron. The truth was that I had flown Spitfires in England and nearly every other type of aircraft then in use, but somehow a Hurricane had never come my way.

I was specially anxious to conceal my inexperience from the squadron — it was bad enough being new to the job and I had the further disadvantage of taking over from Pat Pattle.

Pat was one of the very great air fighters of all time. His

1

exceptional skill had already made him an almost legendary figure. His pre-war record scores against towed targets were the foundation for a deadly accuracy in combat and his perfect flying placed him at an advantage over every opponent. Yet skill and judgment alone do not create either a fighter or a leader — Pat was both. He had the guts of the great warrior with the graciousness which is the hallmark of outstanding leadership. The men would go anywhere with him and his loss weighed heavily on all ranks.

Succeeding Pat would have been difficult for anyone, even under normal circumstances, and my task was even harder. I had come to take over the remnants of a famous fighter squadron which had been cut to pieces in Greece. 33 Squadron had been decimated. Even with the remains of 80 Squadron — our great rivals — we could now only muster some five Hurricanes of which we were lucky to have three serviceable. We had lost all our equipment and spares during the evacuation of Greece a few weeks earlier.

Pat had been killed in a last immortal air battle over Athens as he led a combined force from 33 and 80 Squadrons into action against ten times their number of Germans. He had gone in to shoot a Messerschmitt off the tail of another Hurricane — a typical act. He succeeded too, but the inevitable happened, and a horde pounced on him from behind. It was the only way they could have caught him out — the victor of countless engagements against hopeless odds.

A few days later the squadron had moved to Crete — what was left of it — still fighting. Half the personnel had gone straight back to Egypt where I had the task of reorganising them. The other half had to carry on in Crete. They had done wonders too — eighteen enemy bombers shot down in two short weeks without loss, but it could not go on indefinitely. Pilots and ground crews were exhausted, going from day to day without even a change of clothes, constantly harried by enemy air-raids and operating from dawn to dusk without relief.

I had come over from Egypt with some rested pilots to relieve the hard-pressed garrison who returned in the flying-boat which brought us for some well-earned leave. I found that we were lodgers at Maleme — the little airstrip belonged to the Fleet Air Arm and was commanded by a naval officer — tall, lean Commander George Beale, O.B.E. The remains of a Fleet fighter squadron were also there commanded by Alan Black. They had two or three old Gladiators and a couple of Fulmars. We also had the remains of 30 Squadron with us for a few days — two or three clapped-out old Blenheims which could only just get off the short strip.

With this motley array, we had to defend the west of Crete including the great natural harbour of Suda Bay. With improvised radar warning and fighter control equipment, we had little hope of seriously reducing the scale of enemy attack. We could only nibble at them. The Blenheims and Gladiators were useless against more modern aircraft and the Fulmars would not stand a chance against a Me 109. So the defence of Crete fell to the few Hurricanes of 33 Squadron at Maleme with a few more belonging to 112 Squadron at Heraklion, some seventy miles to the east.

On the ground, the island was full of soldiers. There were more than 30,000 of them, New Zealanders, Australians, British and Greek, but they had very little equipment and most of them were tired and dispirited after the retreat from Greece. Nevertheless, they were a formidable force of magnificent human material and commanded by the famous General Freyberg, V.C. He was reported to be confident of repelling any attempt at invasion even although the enemy did have command of the air.

Meanwhile, in Greece, the enemy's plans for invasion were going forward at an increasing pace. They were mustering 1,500 aircraft to blast us out of existence. A new airfield was coming into commission in the Peloponnese — it would bring us within range of the Me 109s. General Freyberg was expecting the airborne attack in about a week. My plans for reorganising the squadron did not look too hopeful but, as ever, we planned

3

for success. There was no alternative. The few were to fight and go on fighting for time. In time we should have the aircraft we needed, but time was vital. It was a commodity to be bought with all we had. We bought it.

II

I called over one of my newly joined sergeant-pilots and he went over the cockpit with me showing me the position of the various controls. I could not make the radio work, and we spent some time turning the different knobs in vain. In the grey dawn, I noticed that the other two pilots were in their places, sitting quietly in the aircraft, waiting. We were at "stand-by" — ready to take off at a moment's notice.

Suddenly there was the roar of engines starting up. I saw the other two Hurricanes take off in a cloud of dust. I waved the sergeant away and prepared to start the engine. As soon as it kicked, I noticed the fitter pull the starter battery to one side and run; I thought "This is efficiency — they run about their business!" Then I looked up. Through the subsiding dust, I saw the others twisting and turning among a cloud of Messerschmitt 109s. Even as I watched, an enemy aircraft dived into the ground in flames.

I opened the throttle and saw a string of five Messerschmitts coming in over the hill firing at me. It seemed an age before my wheels came off the strip; I went straight into a turn towards the approaching 109s, my wing tip within inches of the ground. The faithful old "Hurrybus" took it without a murmur; the enemy flashed past and I went over instinctively into a steep turn the other way.

My mind was set on practical things. How to get my under-carriage up, the hood closed, the gunsight switched on, the prop into coarse pitch, the firing button on, the engine temperature down. All the time I kept the nose up, straining to gain height to manoeuvre. I found many difficulties. My rear view mirror was not adjusted so that I could see over my tail.

4

This meant that I had to do continuous steep turns with my head back to see what was coming after me. Every time I put my head back, my helmet, which I had borrowed and was much too big for me, slipped over my eyes. Then I could not find the switch to turn on my gunsight. I had to look about inside the cockpit for it. Eventually I found it and saw the familiar red graticule glow ready to aim.

Enemy aircraft kept diving in on me in threes or fives. They were travelling fast and did not stay to fight. They just had a squirt at me and climbed away out of range again. It kept me fully occupied with evasive action. Out of the corner of my eye I saw two aircraft diving earthwards in flames. One was a Hurricane. There was no sign of the other. I was alone in a skyful of Germans.

All of a sudden, the sky seemed to empty of aircraft. There was nobody in my immediate vicinity. I found myself at 4,000 feet over the sea. Five miles to the south was the airfield. Streams of tracers and red Bofors shells were coming up focused on small black specks which were enemy fighters still strafing it fiercely. Four pillars of black smoke indicated the position of burning wrecks on the ground.

Just level with me and about a mile away two 109s were turning in wide line astern formation. I headed in their direction. I cut across inside their turning circle and was soon closing in on them from astern at full throttle. They made no alteration but continued to turn, evidently unaware of my approach. I drew in closer and closer with an eye on my own tail to make sure that I was not jumped. I restrained myself with difficulty. It is only the novice who opens at long range. My own teaching!

I went right in on the tail of the second 109 till I was in close formation on him. I was slightly below him and his slip stream was just above me. I could have lifted my nose and touched his tail with my prop. I dropped a little and pulled up with my sight on his radiator. I pressed the firing switch and the Hurricane shook and shuddered as 10,000 rounds a minute poured from the guns into him. Bits broke away and a white trail burst

5

from his radiator as the coolant came pouring out. He turned slowly to the right in a gentle dive. I was determined to see my first victory confirmed and made the great mistake of following him down. I had no difficulty as he was past taking evasive action and I continued to pour my ammunition into him till I noticed tracer coming past me. The other Messerschmitt was on my tail.

I realised my mistake and pulled quickly up into a turn to port. I flick-rolled over into a steep turn the other way and found myself coming in on the enemy's quarter. I opened up to full throttle and gave him a burst. He dived away to port and I followed, this time with an eye open behind me. The sky was clear. For once the odds were even. He had the faster aircraft and could have pulled steadily away from me. But I kept him turning by firing a short burst every time he went straight.

We screamed down together to water-level. There, he drew very slowly away from me. I was able to judge his range perfectly from the splash of my bursts in the water. I kept him dodging in a cloud of bullets and spray till I ran out of ammunition. He would have difficulty in getting home as we had by this time covered many miles of water to the west, and he was certainly full of holes.

I pulled up and climbed gently to about 6,000 feet on my way home. I was apprehensive of running into more enemy aircraft as I was now without ammunition. As I approached Maleme the Bofors guns started firing and strings of red balls floated gently up towards me. I turned and reduced height keeping a watchful eye on the tracers. It was still unhealthy around there.

I headed east along the coast. In Suda Bay a tanker was ablaze. The bombers had been in again. A huge pall of black smoke drifted away to the west. I skirted the bay to keep clear of our own batteries. Down the coast I knew there was a landing-ground at Retimo. I began to wonder whether I could put the Hurricane down safely in a small field. But I was at home in it. I felt part of it after what we had been through.

6

Below, on a level stretch by the beach, I saw the landing-strip. I flew once across it, low down to look for ditches, and came straight in to land. Undercarriage lights gleamed green, flaps checked firmly and I touched lightly down to a nice short landing. A maintenance party refuelled and rearmed the aircraft, and I took off again soon afterwards for an uneventful trip back to Maleme.

A crowd gathered round me as I taxied in to the refuelling pens. Everyone had assumed that I had been shot down. They had seen my 109 come down and they were delighted that I had opened my score. We had accounted for six Me 109s and had lost the other two Hurricanes, shot down in flames. Sergeant Ripsher had been shot down near the airfield and was credited with two enemy aircraft destroyed. We buried him the next day in a little cemetery by Galatos a few miles down the road. Sergeant Reynish had also accounted for a couple and had baled out of his flaming Hurricane over the sea. We had given him up when he walked in late that evening. He had been two hours in the water and had been picked up by a small Greek fishing-boat. We had also lost one Hurricane on the ground. It had been unserviceable, but could have been flying again within a few hours. Now it was a mass of charred wreckage. We had only one aircraft left. The Fleet Air Arm Squadron had lost their Fulmars, burnt out on the ground, as well as a couple of Gladiators. The prelude to invasion had entered upon its last phase.

III

Group Captain George Beamish visited us before lunch and said some kind words about the morning's work. He was commanding the Air Forces, such as they were, in Crete. I had previously known him in Cairo and I had known him by reputation for years.

George Beamish is a big man. He captained the Irish rugger team on so many occasions that it became practically a family institution, especially since his brothers played in the side with him. As a rugger forward George's name is legendary, and he and his brothers formed a distinctive and outstanding family in the regular pre-war Air Force. Charles was decorated early in the war for his pioneer work with night fighters, and Victor was probably the greatest fighter leader of his generation. He was killed leading the Kenley Wing in 1942.

George Beamish gives people the impression he is pleased to see them; he looks them straight in the eye, and he is a born leader of men. I felt that I should be happy to do anything in the world for him, but found it difficult to say. He said: "You've a man's job ahead of you," and it certainly seemed so.

The appearance of the Me 109s meant that the airfield in the Peloponnese was in operation. The enemy could always send over a screen of fighters to occupy us while his bombers came in unopposed. There seemed to be no way around it. Our landing-strips were too small for the operation of large numbers of aircraft even if we could have them, which we could not. We thought it might be possible to use the airfields only for refuelling and rearming and operate from Egyptian bases. But having to fly all that distance meant that we could still be outnumbered over Crete with ease by a fighter force based close by in the Peloponnese.

I suggested that we should try to intercept the bombers out over the islands before they reached Crete and picked up their fighter escort. Beamish agreed that this might succeed for a time and we intended to try it out when and if we received a few replacements. In the meantime he would arrange for some long range Beaufighters to come over and attack the enemy fighter base. But it was clear that we had not sufficient resources in the Middle East to make any significant reduction to the enemy air effort over Crete. In effect we were a token force, token of the unbreakable resistance of Britain, token of the future, when the position would be reversed. In the meantime our course was clear. We should fight to the end.

Soon after supper the "alert" was sounded. I went down to

the far end of the strip to see how the guards were. As I walked down the road in the darkness I heard an aircraft flying low towards us from the east. It was being fired at and was returning the fire from its nose and tail guns. It was coming straight along the road towards me. I looked hurriedly for a ditch. There was none. So I lay flat on the ground in a slight dip just off the road. Just before it reached the edge of the airfield, the enemy aircraft started dropping a stick of 50-kilo kombs. The thumps of the successive explosions came rapidly nearer. The last bomb went off less than one hundred yards from where I lay, and the splinters screamed across just above my head. The enemy gunners were by then firing at where they thought our aircraft should be so their bursts went wide of the road. They hit nothing, but they caused a good many of us to be thoughtful.

I walked on to where the men were standing in a deep slit trench. I assumed a calm which I did not feel and asked if they were all right. Just then another aircraft approached so I got down in the trench with them, thankful for cover. It came straight at us, low down, firing and dropping bombs. This time I had a rifle, borrowed from one of the guards. We aimed at the shadowy shape as it flashed past over us — like shooting geese in the gloaming on an East Anglian estuary. We fired together and had the great satisfaction of knocking a large piece of cowling off. It clattered to the ground where we later collected it, a battered sheet of metal about three feet square, probably off one of the engines. The aircraft was a Heinkel. The next one came along the road again and we fired at it too. It returned our fire with a vicious burst from the tail gunner. But the shots went wide. Later, when all was quiet, I walked back along the road and met some of the men on their way to inspect the aircraft for damage. We could see nothing in the darkness so we left them till the morning. I was very tired and crept thankfully into bed.

One obvious step to be taken was to try to reduce our aircraft losses on the ground. We put every available man on to digging pits in the hillside to protect the aircraft from splinters and bullets. We shifted tons of earth. Greek labour was brought in to help. But frequent air-raids interrupted the work and we lost another potential Hurricane, burned out on the ground by a lucky hit.

The men were magnificent. They performed miracles with the old wrecks which remained, robbing one to make another serviceable. Soon we had two Hurricanes flying again. The Fleet Air Arm pilots at their own request joined in with us and took their turn on our Hurricanes. We had orders from Egypt to concentrate on enemy reconnaissance aircraft. So we used to take off and patrol over Suda Bay at 24,000 feet when one was plotted coming in. But our ground control was improvised and not very reliable. We made few interceptions.

Two more Hurricanes came in one morning from Egypt. It was a great event. It brought our numbers up to four. The sole remaining Fleet Air Arm Gladiator left for Egypt, but its tired old engine gave out over the sea and the pilot was unfortunately lost with his aircraft.

At Beamish's request I went off one fine morning to inspect the island of Milo, where the famous statue of Venus was found. My interest in the island was not that of the artist so much as to see whether there was any evidence of enemy shipping there and whether an airfield was being constructed. Milo was about twenty minutes' flying away from Maleme. It was a hot hazy day and I was afraid that I might miss the island. But it appeared out of the haze all right and I circled the lovely natural harbour there in search of shipping. The bay was empty, except for a wreck stranded on the beach, a little coaster which was a relic of the evacuation from the mainland. I flew low across the island and could see no trace of an airfield being prepared. People waved to me as I skimmed low across the fields and vineyards.

I headed back out to sea towards Crete again. Suddenly, silhouetted against the dazzling sea, up-sun from me, I saw a single aircraft heading in the opposite direction. It was a three-engined Junkers 52, a German transport aircraft probably returning to Greece from Rhodes. I swung across towards it and came straight in on a quarter attack. Tracers flashed past me from the rear gunner. I fired a long burst as I came in. I was travelling very fast and shot past him under the starboard wing within a few feet of the propeller. I pulled up and round as for a peace-time practice exercise. This time I aimed at his starboard motor. The pilot was by now right down close to the water taking violent evasive action. He was so low that his wheels touched the water at one point throwing up a cloud of spray. My bullets seemed to have no effect, except that the rear gun was now silent. I overshot again and came in for the third time from well astern and more slowly. This time I took the port engine and gave it a steady burst. Flames started to come from the wing-root near the fuselage. I pulled away to port and watched.

The flames grew in size and licked back along the fuselage to the tail. Suddenly the whole aircraft pulled up into a steep climb and turned over on to its back, a mass of flames. It fell back into the water tail first and disappeared straight away. A plume of black smoke drifted away, detached from any source. The water resumed its calm and peaceful appearance. There was no sign of survivors. Like the smoke, I felt strangely detached from the whole episode. I was glad the end had come quickly for them. I always hoped it would be so for me.

I resumed my course for base, climbing steadily and keeping a sharp look-out for enemy aircraft. Crete loomed up ahead, a jagged mountain range rising purple from the vivid blue Aegean to the clear cloudless sky — an exquisite water colour. I thought of Skye and the Cuillin Hills on whose rocks I used to scramble in student days. But this was on a grander scale. The hills stood vast, sharp in shade and colour, a barrier past which the enemy would not pass, though he would linger there for a time.

All of a sudden I caught sight of aircraft below, flashing low across the water in the opposite direction. They were Me 110s. I turned in automatically towards them. They were about two

11

miles away on my starboard bow. The leader saw me coming and jettisoned something which fell into the water throwing up a plume of spray. I had not had time to count how many they were when I realised that the whole sky was full of aircraft. They were in formations of nine and twelve. The nearest were Stukas, level with me and only half a mile away to starboard. I decided to take the nearest and turned in to the attack. Behind me, I noticed an unpleasantly large number of others rapidly approaching.

I opened up to full throttle and closed in fast on the Stukas. They shot at me with their rear guns as I drew in on the tail of the nearest. I concentrated on my sight and on the target now growing rapidly larger within the glowing red ring. As its span seemed to touch the outside ring I pressed the firing button and held the quivering aircraft straight and steady. The rounds poured out from the eight guns, the muzzle flames leaping round the leading edges of the wings. The tracers converged into the target. It seemed an age before anything happened. Then the Stuka flicked rapidly over onto its back and went straight down at the water in a vertical dive.

Tracers were passing me in both directions now and unpleasantly close. I pulled up and away into the sun preparing to fight it out with the Me 109s behind me. But they must have had enough and they were probably getting short of petrol for the return journey. They did not follow me. The air was suddenly empty of aircraft again. I went on homewards. I found I was covered in sweat and a little breathless. My legs felt weak. It was as if I were coming off the field after a hard game of rugger.

I called up the Controller on my radio reporting the movement of large numbers of enemy aircraft in formation in a northerly direction. As it happened, he was well aware of the situation as they had just been blitzed by these same aircraft and had suffered several casualties. He replied to my call and instructed me to land at Retimo and not at Maleme. His voice was deep and guttural and it was not the man who had been on duty when I left. It suddenly crossed my mind that the airborne invasion might have started and that the radio might have been taken over by the enemy. I was determined not to be enticed down at an enemy-controlled airfield. So I replied that I had insufficient petrol and would land at Maleme. This produced an urgent message saying on no account to land at Maleme. Over the airfield I called the fighter "ops" control and was told to look out for enemy fighters. I looked everywhere for signs of Me 109s but there was nothing I could see. So I came in on a very quick turn to land. I nearly touched down with my undercarriage still retracted as the machine was an old one and had a slightly different undercarriage mechanism. I went round again just in time, an easy target for enemy fighters if they had been there.

I taxied in to the pens quickly in case the airfield should be attacked. There, I was reassured. There had been no invasion. My imagination had run riot. There had been a very heavy bombing attack, however, and the usual horde of Me 109s had engaged all three of our available Hurricanes. The Fleet Air Arm boys had been on stand-by and they had fought magnificently and gallantly with ten times their number of Me 109s. They had knocked down at least six but none of them had come back. I was apparently the sole survivor, but one other came limping in much later, full of holes, having had to land at Retimo.

The day's fighting had again reduced our fighting strength to one Hurricane, so our activity was restricted to the interception of enemy reconnaissance aircraft. The bombing and ground strafing attacks were intensified during the days that followed. 30 Squadron took their Blenheims, which were quite useless under these conditions, back to Egypt, leaving behind only ground personnel. We sent a Sunderland full of men back for rest and rekitting. With them went Alan Black who had led his Fleet Air Arm boys so gallantly through these difficult days. He was going to try to get more aircraft.

We had that in mind too. And more aircraft did arrive! One

solitary Hurricane arrived, without warning and not in radio touch, right in the middle of an attack on the airfield. He had his wheels down and was coming in to land when the Messerschmitts picked him up. He was being shot at almost before he realised what was happening. His undercarriage came up and he headed west with a crowd of them buzzing round him. And that was all we saw of him.

The position was virtually untenable from the air point of view. We could not operate with sufficient numbers to be effective nor could we protect our aircraft from being destroyed on the ground. So far as reserves of aircraft were concerned, there were absolutely none in the whole Middle East theatre. It was therefore decided by the Headquarters at Cairo to withdraw such aircraft as remained and attempt to operate from Egyptian bases.

Beamish called me on the phone. "Take your serviceable aircraft to Egypt," he said, naming the airfield to which we were to go. I acknowledged the order and prepared my one Hurricane to leave. There was considerable interest shown in who was to take it. I felt it right to stay with the men. There was one sergeant-pilot of 80 Squadron with us who had somehow got left behind when they had left on their way back from Greece. So I sent him back with many messages for our pilots who were over there. We stayed to face whatever came without aircraft, but still determined to fight.

In the event of invasion, my orders were to put my men in reserve to the 22nd Battalion New Zealand Infantry who were responsible for the ground defence of Maleme. We were to come under the orders of the Colonel commanding the Battalion. I called on him one evening. His headquarters were on the side of a gully in the hill above the airfield. His name was Andrew and he wore the Victoria Cross from the last war. We arranged details together and carried out a trial exercise the following morning to make sure that everything worked smoothly.

The arrangement was that, as soon as an invasion started,

signalised by the arrival of the first enemy parachutist, I should assemble my men at an agreed rendezvous nearby. Here, we were to be met by a New Zealand officer who was to escort us to our position. The location would naturally depend upon the direction of the attack and other factors. It could not be pre-determined. We rehearsed this simple plan without a hitch on the day my last Hurricane left for Egypt. It was the 19th of May 1941. The sands were running out.

II

CRETE — INVASION

I

It was still dark when I woke. I heard voices and movement in nearby tents. The camp was stirring. It was 0530 hours on the 20th of May 1941.

I was very tired. The strain of carrying the Squadron through the past ten days had been heavy. I could have slept for hours. I stretched and grunted and turned out of bed. Myhill, my adjutant, had woken too and we hurriedly pulled on our clothes by torchlight. It was very chilly in the early morning air, and we wore our heavy fur-lined leather flying-jackets and our warm flying-boots.

Outside, men were moving through the darkness towards the gully between two small hills which was our rendezvous and assembly point. As I stumbled through the olive groves and along the side of the hill the silence was profound. The stars twinkled in the immensity of the sky. I wondered at the apparent folly of this early morning activity.

In the gully, the men were huddled together in little groups talking in subdued voices. We checked the numbers and settled down to wait. The routine was to stand by till half an hour after dawn. I chatted to the New Zealand officer who was to show us where to go if anything happened. We had no sense of impending events. If the enemy tried a landing we were ready for him. We were almost regretful that our role was to be "in reserve". Like General Freyberg, we were confident of our ability to hold the island against all comers. We had still to learn our last costly lesson in air power.

The minutes dragged by. We stamped our feet and moved restlessly to keep warm. It was getting light and the sky turned from black to purple, to blue. The landscape came to view. The matchless mountains to the south, dark against the sky. The blue Aegean stretching out to the horizon in the north.

At seven o'clock the stand-by period was over. Just one more routine completed. We were free to go about the business of the day. I dismissed the men and they hurried off to breakfast. I strolled back to my tent wondering if I could snatch some more sleep. The sun was coming up and it was already getting warm. I stripped to the waist and washed and shaved in the basin outside my tent. The cookhouse down the hill was as active as a beehive. Among the trees around me I could see Beale and the others also shaving.

For the heat of the day we wore only shirt and shorts. I was pulling on my shirt when the alarm bell went. "The usual morning blitz," I thought. I strapped on my revolver and took my tin hat and started off for the "ops" room to find out what was on. Someone came running to meet me. "A hundred plus," he reported.

The men were grousing at having their breakfast interrupted. But they were making for the slit trenches which were dispersed throughout the olive grove. We had too much experience of air attacks to take them lightly. I headed for my usual vantage-point, a trench out on the side of the hill overlooking the landing-strip where I could watch the camp and the airfield simultaneously. I found Vernon Woodward and young Dunscombe already there. The trench could hold three at a pinch. It was a good one, deep and narrow.

The air reverberated with the noise of many engines. As yet we could not see them. But slowly it became apparent to me that this was bigger than the usual blitz. Nevertheless I could not believe that it would be more than a blitz. It seemed so suicidal for them to try dropping paratroops in broad daylight on to prepared positions. It was suicidal for many, but I under-estimated the determination of our enemies.

17

In any event our orders were clear. We were not to move till it was apparent that invasion was occurring. So we watched the skies as interested spectators watching the teams come out on the field for a rugger match. The first formations of bombers —Junkers 88s — were in sight now and wheeling in to run up over us. We watched them closely, with a more personal and apprehensive interest now. They were clearly going to pass straight overhead. That meant we were the target. We waited till we heard the whistle and whine of several scores of heavy bombs on their way down, and then we went flat in the bottom of our trench. The bombs struck in twelves, earth spouted to the heavens, the crump and shock of impact crept closer up the hill. The noise was indescribable. The ground shuddered and shook under us as the bomb pattern passed over and beyond.

The whole area was shrouded in thick choking dust, and earth and stones were falling everywhere. We could not see more than a few yards. But we heard the whistle of more bombs on their way down and we kept below ground. The concussion of the bombs bursting close to us shook in the sides of the trench. We were covered in earth. Our eyes and mouths were full of grit. And still it went on. We were shaken by the earth shock till our teeth felt loose and we could hardly see. Debris continued to crash around us and the sides of the trench crumbled. We lost count of time.

There remained the continuous roar of aircraft overhead and the apparently continuous whine of bombs descending. Later these sounds were punctuated by long bursts of cannon and machine-gun fire as low-flying fighters came in to attack the anti-aircraft gunpits. These were already silent under the terrific weight of attack with the exception of one Bofors gun down by the beach. This went on firing for some time till a host of Stukas and Me 109s fastened on it and shot and blasted it out of existence. I remember the sense of admiration for that determined British gun-crew.

It seemed a long time later that I noticed there were no more bombs coming. It was eight o'clock precisely. We could still see

18

nothing beyond a few yards due to the dust. But looking straight up you could see the blue sky. And there, only a few hundred feet above us, were passing packed formations of Junkers 52s. Gliders towed behind were casting off and circling down towards the west. They were to land in a dried river bed about three hundred yards away, a very rough landing, but most of them survived it. Everywhere silhouetted against the blue were parachutes, strings and strings of them, all colours, floating rapidly down among us.

I watched, as if in a dream, as a formation of Ju 52s disgorged their paratroops. My brain seemed numb and unable to appreciate the significance of the scene. The other two with me seemed to be in the same state. Suddenly a gaunt and grimy figure stood on the edge of our trench. It was Beale. Pointing up, he said, "Hadn't you better get your men moving? I am off to the Battalion headquarters to see what I can do for the Colonel." Memory sprang to life with his words. I realised that the long awaited signal had been given. We jumped out of the trench and I sent Woodward and Dunscombe running to collect the men for whom they were responsible. I went also at the run to round up others. Soon I had a number with me, collected from the slit trenches in the middle of the camp. Aircraft were still roaring overhead only a few feet up and they were firing at every sign of movement round us. We kept close to the ground and crept in single file round to the gully.

As we peered through the thick dust from the bombing and picked our way among the shattered olive trees where our camp had stood, there seemed to be a bomb crater at every step. We could see upwards to the blue sky where parachutists still seemed to be coming down everywhere. Suddenly we almost stumbled over the crouched figure of a British soldier. He was bent over an empty oil drum. Inside it was a small stove with a billycan bubbling on it. His grimy face looked up at us. "Like a nice cuppa tea, Sir?" he asked. At that moment the question could not have been more incongruous nor could it have been more welcome! We were parched with thirst, our mouths full of grit. I accepted gratefully and we shared sips of hot sweet tea as the battle continued to rage about us.

We arrived first at the gully and lay in cover waiting for the others to arrive. There was no sign of our New Zealand guide. The trees and tents in the camp had been blown to bits. Great craters gaped everywhere. Dust was still in the air and it lay thick on everything. Our mouths were dry and full of grit and we were covered in dirt. My ears and head were still singing and I was unable to think clearly. I was very frightened, but shame was stronger than fear, and I chatted about trivialities to the men. They too were badly shaken and automatically shrank down as every aircraft went over.

Soon the imperturbable Woody appeared with a few men behind him. He had found difficulty in collecting them as some slit trench areas were cut off by pockets of enemy para-troops. Dunscombe was not long behind him and reported the same thing. We decided to move without waiting further. It was clear that the New Zealanders were fully occupied where they were. At their request, I sent Woody and Dunscombe with some men to prospect to the south. It was the last I saw of them. I led the rest up the hill to the east and found some New Zealanders behind a stone wall. They did not know what was happening elsewhere, so I decided that we should hold this ground against possible attacks from the west.

I tried to remember tactical exercises I had done on Salisbury Plain. I made a quick survey of the ground and posted the men behind good natural cover to command the best field of fire. Others now arrived with Myhill in charge and I appointed him to command one sector, while Sergeant-Pilot Butterick took over the other sector. Both men were cool and capable and ready for anything. I walked from one end of our line to the other, gratified to find my brain working clearly again and the sense of fear gone. Aircraft still roared overhead and bullets kicked up the dirt, but I was too busy to worry about them.

Through the lifting haze, gliders could still be seen coming down in the river bed in the valley below. Figures ran from them into nearby cover. To the north, a huge formation of Ju 52s was dropping more paratroops. Everywhere, the sky was busy with aircraft. I decided it was time to contact the Colonel and report my action to him. I left Myhill in charge and walked round the hillside to the headquarters. More paratroops were being dropped to the east round Galatos. Bullets from various sources still whined past and there was still the occasional crump of a bomb. But the blitz had lifted and the land battle was on.

The Colonel's headquarters seemed to have stayed outside the heavily bombed area. The leaves were still on the trees and the dust was less thick. I found Beale there with the Colonel. My mouth was still full of grit so I asked for water. The Colonel was sorry, there was no water handy, but there was beer in the mess. The "mess" was a circle of sandbags with an upturned crate as a table. We strolled over to it as I told him what I had done with my men. He approved of my action. He himself had still no word from his forward platoons and we did not know how the attack was developing.

We sat and opened a couple of bottles. They must have been the last on the island. As we drank thankfully, there was a crack from the bank behind us and the dirt flew where a bullet had struck. A few moments later there was the same whine and crack. Someone was trying to pick us off where we sat. I became apprehensive. But the Colonel said: "Let us finish our beer," so we sat on. I hurriedly finished mine off and waited for him. He rose leisurely and we strolled back into the headquarters dugout. I was glad to be inside.

I found Beale wondering about the safety of our respective orderly rooms. They had instructions to burn documents in the event of attack, but it looked as though the paratroops might have dropped there too soon. The cypher books were in the charge of two officers of 30 Squadron. Ours had been burned in the retreat from Greece. We hoped that they would be safe and there was nothing to be done about them. But we decided to try to reach the orderly room at the airfield headquarters just to make sure of the destruction of the files and records. Also I hoped to be able to pick up some of our men who had been cut off in that area.

II

Three of us set off from the Battalion headquarters. Colonel Andrew had decided to come with Beale and me to see how his own forward elements were faring. We walked up over the crest of the hill together. On the far side, we found a little group round a badly wounded soldier. He had been hit in the lungs and was coughing blood. He was pretty far gone. Three of his pals were round him holding his hand as he prepared to make his last journey. We left them and went on down the hill into the olive grove. At the end of the gully there should have been an advanced post of New Zealand infantry. Their trenches were empty. The Colonel decided to go back to his headquarters and await runners from his companies.

Beale and I walked on, keeping in cover as far as we could. There was intermittent fire coming from down on our left where the glider troops were forming up after landing in the river bed. We kept out of sight of them as we moved across the face of the hill. We came to a coloured parachute. There was nothing tied to it and there was no one in sight. But I had a hunch the place was unhealthy and we went back a few yards. Here we found a slit trench with two airmen in it. They had rifles. We took them with us and went forward again. Beale was in the lead. I followed with my revolver ready. Then came the two airmen. We crept quietly forward.

All of a sudden Beale pitched forward about five paces with a cough and grunt. He had been hit in the stomach. Fortunately the bullet came out between his ribs without damaging his vitals. But he and we were not to know that. I leant over him, speechless in stupid concern. There was nothing I could say, so I said, "Are you all right?" — a ridiculous question under the circumstances. The idea was in my mind that he had been hit by a stray bullet from an aircraft, so I was not taking any special precautions myself.

As I uttered the words, however, I felt a tremendous blow on my left shoulder. It picked me up off my feet and spun me in the air. My right arm flung out and was also struck violently. I found myself on the ground. My left shoulder was quite numb and blood was spouting from my right fore-arm where the artery had been cut. I had been hit by two tommy-gun slugs from a nearby paratroop. He had also hit one of the airmen a glancing blow on the ribs with another slug.

We were all flat on the ground now and in cover from further fire for the moment. My arm was a nasty sight. Part of my forearm had been carried away as the slug spread on the bone and tore it out. I found it difficult to move myself as neither arm could be of any help. Beale struggled over to me. One airman came with him. Together they took out a field dressing and tied it on my arm by the elbow. They started to tighten it up with the help of a stick to make the tourniquet effective. As they tightened it, however, the stick broke.

In the meantime, bullets were whining past us again. We were in an unhealthy position. There was not time to do more. So my tourniquet was left as it was. An extraordinary thing was that it was just tight enough to slow up the flow of blood from my artery enough to let it clot and so stop, without being so tight as to stop the blood supply to the rest of my arm. As the tourniquet remained on for three days that fact saved me from losing either my life or my arm.

The others decided to crawl back to the gully, where they would be under cover again to walk back to our lines. I was unable to crawl as both my arms were broken. So they helped me to my feet and I started to run back across an open stretch to where there would be cover to walk. It was about a hundred yards. I set my teeth and ran. The bones ground together with a sickening noise as my helpless arms flapped about. The pain was excruciating. When I had only about five paces to go, I relaxed the attention which had been focused completely on my objective. The result was a blackout. I fainted and fell, just short of cover, in the open, exposed to fire from two enemy positions.

I was oblivious to the passage of time. The next thing I knew was that Beale and the airmen were beside me. They lifted me up. I made a supreme effort of concentration and tried to walk. I was half carried to a place a few yards away where a tent had stood before the blitz. It was dug into the hillside and afforded good cover. I watched a stick grenade or explosive shell pitch five yards ahead of us. The dirt flew and the explosion cracked on us, but miraculously no one was touched by splinters.

They laid me down on my back in the pit and sat close in to review the position. Beale's face was white and haggard. His wound kept him bent almost double with pain. Only his amazing spirit kept him going. He was determined to reach our lines. He promised to send a rescue party to bring me in and set off on his own. He got back all right only to be taken prisoner later when the aid post where he was being attended to was overrun. A rescue party, led by one of my own officers and made up of airmen, counter-attacked and reached me. But they found me unconscious in a pool of blood. My right arm lay across my stomach from which the blood appeared to have come. I was covered in flies and without sign of life. They left me for dead and later reported to Cairo that I had been hit in the stomach.

In fact, I was far from dead. I was conscious much too frequently for pleasure. Shortly after Beale left I had sent one of the airmen back by an alternative route. The other had sat by me as I reviewed the situation. I was very weak and blood was still welling from my shoulder and arm. It could only be a matter of time. I had an acute thirst from the loss of blood, aggravated by the hot Mediterranean sun which blazed down from a cloudless sky. I had no water. I decided to hasten the end. I had no thought for the future. Death for me was an end of everything. Above all it was an end to my present extreme discomfiture. The airman had my revolver. I told him to give it to me. He put it into my left hand which was lying helpless on my chest. I made a terrific effort of concentration and got the muzzle under my chin. But the strength to pull back the hammer had left my fingers. The airman was shocked and took the gun from me. I asked him to shoot me but he was clearly horrified at the idea. So I gave up and sent him off to try to get back to our lines. He and the other man were captured on their way.

The sun beat down from the blazing sky. My thirst was extreme. I was so weak that I could not twitch a finger. The flies crawled over my face undisturbed. Clouds of them gathered around me, attracted by the pool of blood in which I lay. Big shiny black flies. They saved my life. They laid eggs in my wounds. Later I was crawling with maggots. The maggots ate the decaying flesh and prevented gangrene. But at the time the flies were the last torment. Tortured with pain and thirst I lay in the sun with a deep desire for death.

Time passed slowly. I was intermittently conscious. Sometimes conscious of noise as machine-guns rattled nearby. Always acutely conscious of thirst. I craved for water as I had never before craved for anything. Some say that, faced with death, the past comes before the fading gaze in shifting scenes. I had no such experience. I was alone and dying from loss of blood and thirst. It was a race to see which won. I only desired the race to end.

My hopeless frame of mind was strange. I had been born and brought up in a Scottish manse in the best tradition. I had had every chance to know better, but I had long preferred to believe that there was no God. I had long scoffed at the things I had been taught to revere as a child. I had long been accustomed to run my own life my own way. I had done what I wanted, up to the limit of my ability. And now it was the end. I only wanted the end to come quickly. For once my desires were being thwarted.

Night came and it was cold. Bitterly cold. But thirst was still

25

the primary consideration. I was crazy with thirst. There was nothing in my power that I would not have done for a drink of water. But there was nothing I could do. I just lay.

Sometime that night (or was it the next night?) I heard machine-gun fire close beside me. I could hear men talking in German. Then there was the sound of men running past me. And the gun started to fire again — this time on my other side. Another pause, and it opened up still further away. Then it came closer and past me again. It was an old ruse. One gun-crew giving the impression of many. Later I heard that the Germans had only twenty-seven men that night and were reinforced at dawn. A platoon might have saved Crete if they had known.

The sun blazed down again. I had lost all sense of time. I must have been unconscious for most of that day and the following night. On the third day I had a spell of consciousness again. There were men passing just by me. I tried to croak at them. They saw that I was alive and came round me. Six young German paratroops. My tongue was dry and swollen. They saw my need and produced their water-bottles. The first drops to pass my throat were more precious to me than life. I drank and drank. I seem to remember draining many water-bottles. Someone had cold tea with brandy in his. Another gave me some dried fruit from a cellophane packet. I was sick. And drank again. "Water" was the only word I could whisper through my cracked lips. Someone pulled a blanket over me and I was alone again. Only the craving for water remained.

I remember being carried in on a stretcher. We were passing the old headquarters. Every lurch of the stretcher was agony. I passed out again into merciful oblivion. Then I was lying among a crowd of other wounded and dying men in the village street. There was someone close by me on either side. One was silent, he was dead. The other was one of my own airmen. I was delirious. I heard afterwards that I kept saying, "It's all right, chaps. You will all be all right. Just stay where you are and do what I tell you." I was reliving the battle on the hillside. Soon I

26

was carried into a little shop on the village street. Here, Flying Officer Tom Cullen was doing the work of ten men. He had dysentery when the blitz came and crawled out of bed to attend to the wounded. He was the only medical officer at Maleme. Having established an aid post on the hillside he worked there under fire while the battle raged round them. Then they were overrun by the enemy and he was taken prisoner together with his wounded men and transferred to the village.

Now he was attending to all the wounded as they were brought in. He had been on his feet for three days and nights. And his only helpers were untrained men. My fitter sergeant from 33 Squadron was helping in the "operating theatre". The intelligence officer from 30 Squadron was his anaesthetist. I was put on a table, only half-conscious. A piece of torn parachute fabric was laid across my face and ether poured on to it till I passed right out. Cullen then operated on my shoulder and cleaned up and bandaged both wounds.

I came to in the street again. I had one idea still predominant in my mind — water. Someone filled a water-bottle and laid it on my chest. By moving two fingers I could tip it up so that it poured into my mouth. The water was like wine. I gulped greedily.

Later I was carried into another little house on the side of the street. I remember an earth floor, one small window, and an open door. I was placed on a wooden bench inside, still with a water-bottle on my chest. I kept on calling for it to be refilled. There was a constant stream of wounded through the little door. Soon they were everywhere inside. There was no room to walk between bodies on the floor.

Night came and darkness added horror to the scene. Men were groaning and crying out. Men were dying. Men were bleeding and being sick over each other. The sounds and smells were indescribable. But one thing remained priority — water. Someone refilled my water-bottle at intervals.

Soon we had run out of good water. The water became impossible to drink due to the chlorine in it. It was acid and

27

made you immediately sick. Someone found a barrel of sweet Samos wine and broached it. Thereafter we drank Samos and water mixed. It was just possible to get it down. But the result was that everyone became intoxicated. The last vestiges of control vanished.

In the morning they came and carried out the dead. Someone came up to me and said, "How do you feel?" I heard but was too weak to answer. Later there was a stab in the arm as I was given a huge shot of dope. I was carried out into the open. Strapped on my stretcher to a motor-cycle sidecar I was driven to the airfield.

I remember nothing of the drive. The next time I was conscious, I was lying on my stretcher on the airfield. There was the familiar smell of petrol and exhaust fumes, with the peculiar odour of aircraft paint. A Junkers 52 was standing close by. Others were scattered about. The place was packed with planes.

I was picked up and carried to the Ju 52. As the stretcher was being manœuvred through the door, my left arm was caught by the side. The shock pierced through my semi-conscious mind. I cried out with the pain.

They laid me in the cabin. The engines started and we took off without delay as our own guns were shelling the airfield and it was unhealthy to linger. There were only two others in the plane with me apart from the crew. One was a New Zealand officer who had half his arm blown off. The other was a corporal whose face was missing. Bloodstained bandages covered what was left of him.

Our wheels left the ground and I felt the aircraft turn immediately out to sea. Otherwise it would have run into our own machine-gun fire. We headed away north low over the water. The lower half of the German gunner as he sat at his post was all that I could see.

Later the incongruity of it all struck me. One day shooting down a Junkers 52 and a few days later travelling in one as a passenger. One day being shot at by Germans, the next being carried by them. One day eager to live, the next anxious to die. Life was full of apparent contradictions. Although I was too far gone to realise it, there had been an interesting series of coincidences: my being sole survivor in air combat twice running; the amazing coincidence of the tourniquet being adjusted to a nicety; these were links in a chain of evidence that was to have a profound influence upon my future.

Also, although again I did not realise it, I was on the first plane to evacuate British wounded from Crete. My early evacuation meant that I reached hospital in time to save my life. It was to be touch and go, but I should live again. The fact that I was a prisoner had hardly crossed my mind. I was already a prisoner to myself. My mind was imprisoned in my own affairs. I thought only of myself and my immediate surroundings. The Junkers was carrying me to total captivity.

III

The engines shut off to a tick-over. There was the familiar bump and rattle as we hit the ground and tore across the rough surface to a standstill. We had landed at an airfield outside Athens. It seemed as though my wounds were redhot. Every movement of the aircraft as it taxied across the field was agony. I fainted.

Then there was the lorry with its flapping canvas hood closed at the back. There was a cloud of dust as we rattled off down the bumpy Greek roads to the city. It was stiflingly hot. The corporal with the bloodstained bandages on his face was groaning. He was nearly gone and his passing was painful.

The New Zealand officer was also beside me. I remember the sight of his face, grimy and white at the lips, with teeth set hard. Every lurch of the lorry moved my arms. The vibration shook the shattered flesh and bones. I cried out. Mercifully I was only partly conscious.

I remember sunny streets seen through a slit in the canvas. Then I was lying on a paved stone floor in the entrance of the prisoner-of-war hospital. Someone asked in English for my name. As I was speechless, they looked at my bloodstained identity discs. I was carried away. Weeks later, I was to discover that my desert boots which had been tied to my stretcher had been stolen with my stockings and wallet. I was left wearing a pair of blood-soaked shorts, and my identity discs.

When I regained consciousness, I found myself in a bed between sheets. They felt smooth and cool on my skin. It was quiet in the ward. People were talking in low voices nearby. There was no sudden rush and roar of aircraft overhead. Or stutter of machine-gun fire. The crump of high explosive seemed far away.

My wounds were burning and I was still craving for water. Someone put a glass to my lips and cold water trickled deliciously over my parched tongue. I asked for more. And more. I disposed of a huge glass jug full every few hours for the next three weeks.

A doctor was attending to my neighbour. Soon it was my turn. He glanced at my wounds and asked some questions. I was unaware of question or answer. I had no sense of being a prisoner. My doctor was an Australian and the people round me were British. There were no Germans in sight. The world was bounded by the limits of my bed. It was a painful world to live in, and I would much rather have died. I was in pain and thirsty and tired, and only intermittently conscious. I slept and drank, and slept again. Life was pain and water. And death was sleep. And sleep was good.

ATHENS — PRISONER OF WAR

I

Blair Hughes-Stanton bent over me. He had a glass of water in his hand. I was immediately interested — in the water. Blair was an artist. He had been a camouflage officer with the army in Greece. When the evacuation came he had been taken prisoner. In a temporary prison-camp at Corinth conditions had been bad. There had been a good deal of shooting. Atrocity stories from Crete were circulating among the German guards. Until they were disproved, they were an excuse for reprisals. Blair had gone too near the wire to pick up an orange thrown in by a Greek civilian. The guard had shot him.

So he was in hospital and lucky to be alive. The bullet had entered just below his jaw bone and passed through his palate and teeth, coming out through his cheek the other side. His face and mouth were a mess. And his jaws were wired together so that he could not speak properly or eat at all. He had to be fed on liquids for months. One of the familiar sights in the ward was Blair mashing up some fruit till it could pass through his teeth. He was very good to me. He supplied me with water at regular intervals for days and weeks, and he wrote my letters for me, through the Red Cross, to tell my father and mother that I was alive.

Through him, I began to realise my surroundings. He described the set-up. We were in a prison-camp on the outskirts of Athens. The hospital building had been a school. It was a huge, modern, white concrete building high on the hillside between Piraeus and Athens. The district was called Kokinia.

The hospital was surrounded by barbed wire and had the usual German guard commanded by an SS corporal. Nominally, the corporal came under the orders of a German doctor who was in charge of the unit. Actually, it was he who dictated and interpreted policy relating to our treatment as prisoners. The doctor merely interested himself in our treatment as wounded. Even in this he took little part, as the hospital arrangements and surgery were run by an Australian Major called Brooke Moore, aided by a staff of Australian and British doctors and male medical orderlies.

The building could have accommodated about five hundred beds with reasonable efficiency. As it was, there were far more wounded than could be comfortably handled. At one time there were men lying in the passages and the beds were crowded together in the wards with little space between them. The kitchen facilities were inadequate for these numbers in spite of the extreme shortage of food.

Under these very difficult circumstances, Brooke Moore and his men did a wonderful job. Many of them had volunteered to stay behind to look after the wounded when Greece was being evacuated and heavy casualties were expected from the beaches. All the nurses and many of the doctors had been evacuated to Egypt leaving two skeleton-staffed hospitals behind. One was the Fifth Australian General Hospital, and the other was the Twenty-sixth British General Hospital. The Germans had taken them over and moved them to their present locations, the Australians at Kokinia and the British in the Polytechnic building in Athens. All captured medical personnel were sent to these hospitals and their staffs grew. The casualties from the Greek beaches had been miraculously light, but the hospitals were needed for the stream of wounded which poured in from Crete.

The day after I was brought in, I was carried off to the operating theatre where a British surgeon, Major Harvey, dealt with me. After the operation, I found myself back in the ward and Blair was by my side as usual with water. My thirst was still insatiable. My arms had been dressed and there was a half plaster on my right arm. They told me that my left shoulder was shattered and the humerus fractured near the joint; half of my right forearm was missing including about two inches of the radius, but they hoped that amputation would not be necessary. Like most of the other wounded from Crete, I was in an advanced state of sepsis and shock, and there were maggots in both my wounds. I was very weak and few thought that I would survive. The days went by in procession as in a dream. I had no energy to talk or look around me, I only wanted water and oblivion.

Some days later, I was moved to another part of the ward so that my left arm could have room to be put into a "Thomas" splint. Here, it was not easy for Blair to continue to nurse me. In the next bed there was a French pilot who had been shot down over Crete. His name was Jacquier. He took over the task of nursing me.

Flight-Lieutenant Paul Jacquier was one of the finest men I had ever met. He had been serving in Syria when the French collapse came, and he escaped to Egypt and volunteered to fly with the R.A.F. He was appointed to command a flight in one of our desert fighter squadrons. From there he flew over to Crete while the land battle was in progress and attacked enemy aircraft in the air and on the ground at Maleme. He had been hit by flak and his engine stopped. So he had to put his Hurricane down in a crash landing. He was only slightly injured, but had been picked out of the crash by the Germans.

He spent his days in the service of the wounded. Others who were also convalescent used to go up to the roof to bask in the sun and play cards and read. But not Jacquier. He was constantly moving about the ward with the orderlies, a stalwart quiet figure with a pleasant smile for everybody. Someone's glass was empty. Jacquier would refill it without waiting to be asked. To me, he was always available when I needed him. The flies were bad and kept settling on my face. Jacquier would wave them off. He washed me and shaved me and kept me clean. He encouraged me to eat what there was to eat, and saw that I got fruit from the canteen.

One day, after about three weeks, the guards came in with the news that he was to be taken off by air to Germany. The story went round that he was going to be handed over to Vichy to be shot as a traitor to discourage the other Fighting French as he was the first, or one of the first, of them to be taken prisoner. He received the news with calm, concerned mainly that I should be cared for by someone else. He went to the priest first thing in the morning, as usual. Later that day they came to take him away. He was ready. He said good-bye to me and gave me a private message for his wife. They had been married in Cairo only a few weeks before he was shot down. Then he walked out with his head held high and a smile and a wave for us all — a great gentleman. Fortunately, the stories were false and he was only destined for a prison-camp in Germany.

II

By this time, one of my own officers had arrived in from Crete. He was not wounded but had been brought over with suspected malaria. In fact, there was little the matter with him. His name was Butcher, and he became my nurse and close friend during the critical weeks which followed.

The officers' ward was on the top floor of the hospital. It was in two halves connected by a single door. Each half was about fifteen paces long by six across, with the windows high up in the walls. Lying in bed, you could see only the sky through them. For three months my vision was bounded by these four walls.

Each half of the ward had about thirty beds crowded into it. I was at one end, my left arm stretched out in a splint, the end of which was tied to the wall for support. My right arm was now in a full plaster which had a window cut in it over the forearm to allow the pus to flow out from the gaping festering wound. I was flat on my back and only able to move my legs, and I remained in that position for three months. A steady flow of pale yellow-green pus ran from my shattered shoulder and trickled down towards the back of my neck where it formed a pool, and slowly soaked through the stinking mattress. In those early days, most of my time was spent in a semi-conscious stupor. I was chiefly aware of the agony of daily dressings and the sickly sweet odour of pus, to which I never became wholly reconciled.

As the weeks went by, my physical condition improved slowly and I began to take more interest in my surroundings. Butch moved into the bed next to me. He was my constant companion and sat by me, fed, washed and shaved me. He brushed off the flies and held cigarettes for me so that I could start to smoke again.

I used to suffer a good deal of pain. In addition to my wounds, sores appeared to add to my discomfiture. There were bed sores where my hip bones protruded sharply through the emaciated skin, and others where the plaster pressed on my arm. I had as many as eight at one time on my right arm. One was very painful and exposed the bone at my elbow; there was another between my thumb and first finger and some also appeared on my left arm where it was supported in the "Thomas" splint. All were infected and festering.

The pain from these sores, particularly over the joints, where the nerves are most closely concentrated, drove me almost demented. I was given morphia every four hours by day and twice by night to keep me quiet. Morphia was a great relief. I used to get to the point where self-control was on the verge of complete collapse and I should have become a screaming demented creature. Then I would get an injection and hold on for the last few minutes of agony. Soon a calm would begin to creep over the body, starting at the legs. The muscles which were taut would relax. The wave of relaxation would creep up and flow into the arms. The pain vanished. The mind became calm and peaceful, at rest.

I had morphia for several weeks. But it had its disadvantages.

It is habit forming, like smoking. The more you have the more you want. And if it is not administered carefully the patient gets a craving for it and cannot do without it. I found the effect diminishing to the point where an injection hardly affected me. I suspect that my doctors decided I had had enough and they broke off the treatment gently, administering weaker and weaker doses. Finally it may have been water they gave me for all the effect it had.

But I was still suffering great pain and was given opiates to drink instead. One in particular gave me wonderful relief, even more complete than the morphia. I continued with it for several weeks. Then I decided to stop and broke myself of the habit. By this time the pain was very much reduced and I had little trouble.

Certain incidents and people stand out in the memory of these days. There were a number of Greek officers with us at that time. Later they were moved to a Greek hospital. Michel Vanvakas was in the bed on my immediate right. He had been hit by shrapnel and was wounded all over. His dressing took an hour. It was a painful hour, but he was very courageous. He would clench his teeth silently as the dressings were ripped off. Like me, he stank of stale pus. He became a firm friend. Although we spoke little we suffered much in common. I discovered that an old friend of mine had been billeted in his home near Khania. We conversed in French. I missed him when they carried him away to the Greek hospital.

Opposite us were two Greeks with serious stomach wounds. One had already turned a terrible green colour. He died one night. The other lived through painful days and nights and groaned and grunted and screamed until he too was taken away. His dressing was a daily ordeal for the orderlies. Tough as they were, the stench was overwhelming. They wore masks for the job.

But the majority of the patients had fairly simple wounds. Commander George Beale was there; his clean bullet hole had healed up nicely and he was among the first to be moved to

Germany. There were many broken legs and arms. And a few who had nothing worse than mild dysentery. We had all types.

There was a huge Maori officer who was very seriously wounded. He had led a bayonet charge in Crete for which the Maoris would long be remembered. But they had suffered heavy casualties. This officer had been hit all over by machine-gun bullets. Greatly beloved by his men, he was visited daily by a stream of Maoris who hobbled in to see him from all parts of the hospital. He lasted for weeks and months. His huge frame shrank. He pined slowly away until he was just a bag of tormented bones. He used to scream out in the night, demented with pain. Drugs ceased to help him. At last he died.

Near him was an officer of the Royal Marines. He too had been hit by machine-gun fire in Crete. With both thighs broken he had lain helpless in the open for six days before he was picked up. It was amazing that he had survived. He lay in the ward, very weak, with both legs trussed up in splints. Steel pins through his shins were the anchorage of cables which passed over pulleys at the foot of the bed. Heavy weights attached to these stretched his legs out to help the bones to re-unite.

Owing to his condition, this treatment, which was normal for fractured femurs, was too harsh. The pins in his legs festered. His wounds remained open and discharging. Bed sores appeared too rapidly to be dealt with and became huge open ulcers. He became covered with sores. The inadequate diet did not help matters. He became thinner and thinner until he was just a skeleton. His mind began to crack under the terrific strain. At the end of the fourth month he too died.

I reflected on these things. The Maori and the marine were, on the surface, as tough a pair of warriors as one could ever wish to meet. They had great qualifications for leadership too. They had courage, guts, initiative and thought for their men. And yet, in spite of all that, they lacked something. They had lasted far longer than most men, but in the end it was that something that let them down. They threw the sponge in mentally before they finally collapsed physically. Although I

37

was blind to it myself, that was also what I was doing and what most men in our condition did.

The drama of their passing was pathetic and tragic in the extreme. Psychologically it was interesting. Under the stimulus of physical pain, thought processes became more and more self-centred to an extent depending on either the intensity or the duration of the stimulus. The average person could only stand a certain amount of pain without becoming absorbed in it. A small persistent pain had the same effect in the long run as an intense but short-lived one.

Resistance to pain seemed to vary widely as between individuals. Some were affected quickly and easily. Others, like the Maori and the marine, lived through months of agony. It was easy to say that people were just made like that. But it was not the whole truth. Was there not a spirit which would enable men to rise above circumstance however terrible, and remain masters of themselves and benefactors to others? What was the secret of the heroes and the martyrs through the ages? Was there some supernatural force which could supply what even the strongest person lacked? I pondered on these things as the days dragged by. I saw myself slipping further and further into the bog of self-concern. I was more and more a prisoner to myself.

Although we were wounded and prisoners-of-war, we were typical of many ordinary citizens who, suffering some hurt, are imprisoned by self-concern about it. The hurt can be physical — illness or injury. It can also be mental like bereavement, or unemployment, or some human relationship which has gone wrong, causing fear or bitterness or hurt pride.

Whatever it is, it is something which tends to occupy the mind. People become worried, self-concerned, prisoners to their problems. Their ability to serve the community is instantly affected. Their work suffers, their relationships with other people are impaired. They are not free to give themselves either to people or to things. They become selfish in other ways too, claiming compensations, rights and privileges

38

at the expense of service and duty. Countless man-hours are lost to industry and countless relationships become embittered and broken. A moral and spiritual force which could deal effectively with self-concern would be priceless, not only to individuals, but also to nations. I needed that force desperately but it was to be many months before I would try to find it.

III

Life in the ward was extremely monotonous. We would wake fairly early. The fitter patients would go off and wash and shave. The orderlies came round with a basin of water and I would get my face and hands washed. The guards came round and checked the roll. After this there was a long pause. Then great activity as breakfast arrived.

Breakfast consisted of a half-slice of Greek brown whole-meal bread and a mug of ersatz coffee. The bread was dry or had some sour type of jam on it. The coffee was made from roasted acorns ground up. It tasted quite distinctly of something but it was not coffee. There was, of course, neither milk nor sugar in it. To begin with, I only craved for water, and ate a little fruit. Later I took my share of what was going. Sometimes Butch would be able to buy me some grapes in the canteen. Fruit was pretty plentiful in Greece during that first summer of occupation. But bread was already scarce and we could not purchase it.

After breakfast there was another long pause. A further commotion announced the arrival of the doctors for their rounds. This was the interesting part of the day. Those who waited to be dressed watched the fate of those being dressed with interest, not unmixed with apprehension. It was like waiting to bat at cricket, and watching the rest of the team being bowled out one by one. Sometimes a patient would cry out in pain, and all of us, waiting our turn, would squirm and wonder if we should be able to remain silent when our time came. Some, whose dressings had become a matter of routine, would lose interest and regard the whole thing as a trifling incident in a long and dreary day. But I was not to reach this happy position for nearly eight months.

The morning was a disturbing time for many reasons. First, the threat of dressings was never far removed. I was at the end of the ward and the last to be done. Then there were the men who swept and cleaned the ward who came round and made noises round the bed with their brushes and pails. And the canteen purchases were arranged then too. One of the convalescent patients would come round with a list taking orders for the canteen. Then he would disappear and reappear later with a boxful of stuff. Some days there would be grapes for sale. Others there would be melons, or pears, or oranges. For a time we could buy a few onions. Sliced up they put flavour into our bread.

Lunch was the next great event. It consisted of a plate of hot "soup". This thin washy water had beans floating in it and sometimes a trace of horse meat. With it, we would have another half-slice of bread. Usually it would be dry bread as we were only allowed one helping of white lard each day and this was most often reserved for the evening meal. The "specials", like myself, who were seriously ill, could have some coarse rice pudding to feed us up. I always accepted this and passed it on to Butch who had a healthy appetite and was able to get it down. I would eat a few grapes in lieu.

The afternoon was a time for rest. The healthier patients went out on to the flat roof where they lay in the sun reading or dozing. I just lay. Sometimes I slept when the pain was less acute than usual. I had a fever for those first three months which did not drop below 100 degrees and went as high as 104 degrees at times. It made one content just to lie quietly. There was no energy to spare for any other activity.

Between five and six we began to look out for our evening meal. This consisted of another half-slice of bread with or without lard according to whether we had eaten it earlier or not. There was also another mug of ersatz coffee.

The calorific value of this diet was about 1,200 calories a day. The basic minimum for a man in bed is 2,000 calories, and a man engaged on manual labour requires as much as 5,000 calories per day. So it will be seen that we were on a starvation diet. In fact, had it not been for the Greek Red Cross, we should not have survived these early months in Athens. They managed to supplement our diet with a lorry load of foodstuffs once a week. How they did it, in spite of the terrible conditions prevailing in Athens at that time, is a remarkable story of Greek devotion to Britain. The head of the Red Cross was Madame Zannas. Helping and often accompanying her was Alexandra Poumpoura. I remembered their names and what an encouragement it was when they visited us.

Madame Zannas and her helpers were tireless in their efforts to procure food and comforts for us. Our doctors said that every man who spent more than two months as a prisoner in Greece owed his life to their efforts. Sometimes they were allowed to come into the wards and speak to us. They were always accompanied by Germans to see that they could not give us news or unauthorised gifts. We greatly appreciated all that they were doing for us.

It was September before our own Red Cross parcels started to arrive. From then on we were able to make the diet up to the minimum necessary for health. No one can overestimate the service rendered by the Red Cross in wartime. Our parcels were more than comforts. They were our means of survival and they were a great link with home. It was a pleasure just to read familiar labels on the tins. They were also the best possible propaganda for Britain. Indirectly, they demonstrated to the German guards the falsity of their own propaganda which was describing the serious food situation in Britain. The only real tea and coffee they had seen for years was that contained in our parcels.

Under these conditions it is little wonder that much of the conversation in the ward used to centre around the topic of food. Butch and I developed a game in which we would make believe that we were going out to lunch or dinner. The conversation would run along these lines: "Where shall we dine to-night, Butch?"

"Let's go to Jimmy's," he would reply, referring to a well-known restaurant in Cairo. We would then proceed to order our lunch or dinner or whatever it was. The technique applied equally easily to breakfast. As we described what we were going to eat, a chorus of protests would come from the rest of the ward until finally we would have to desist. The conversation would then change slightly to reminiscences of dinners we had eaten, or the best restaurants for this and that, until it in turn was silenced by the protests of the others whose mouths were watering through our vivid descriptions.

Although this was one of the few games I was able to play, all sorts of entertainments developed. People became ingenious in the art of passing time. Many played cards and bridge schools sprang up everywhere. One of the doctors was an international bridge player and he took classes. Others started handiwork. With a penknife and a piece of wood, works of art began to be created. Some artists began painting or drawing with materials provided by the Greek Red Cross. Books were at a premium. The Greek Red Cross collected English books for us to add to the hospital library. These were censored and passed on to us. Even the most ancient volumes were read with tremendous interest, however obsolete their theme or presentation. I was unable to join in any of these pursuits. Reading was impossible as I could not hold a book or turn the pages.

A really first-class concert party was formed in the hospital. Surprising talent was unearthed in the form of singers, instrumentalists and comedians. Sometimes they would come round the wards in the evening. A Welsh trio sang exquisitely. A London bus driver developed into a comic genius whose repartee and behaviour were a constant source of entertainment and delight. He lived his part all the time and stories of his outrageous behaviour and remarks went round the wards daily.

Butch and I kept trace of all the airmen in the hospital. We used to divide up our prisoner-of-war pay between them. As prisoners, officers were paid and other ranks were not. The theory was that other ranks would earn money by working, which the officers were not allowed to do. But in prisoner-of-war hospitals the men could not work and therefore received no pay. They could only purchase from the canteen if they sold their belongings or were given money by their officers. It was a bad system.

Our airmen were in all stages of health. Some were desperately ill with very serious wounds. Others were relatively slightly injured. As they became fit they would be transferred to a camp nearby from whence they were shipped on to Germany via Salonika. Those who were fit enough to do so, used to visit me regularly and sit by my bed for an hour or so chatting. Later, some of them took on the job of nursing me. They were faithful friends.

Others used to come and sit by me too. One day, soon after I arrived in the hospital, I noticed a vaguely familiar face. I had met Ian Macphail years before, in 1937, in my own home. He was then back from his farm in New Zealand and staying with his mother near us. I was on short leave. He had come to tea with my brother. Now, four years later, after Butch went to Germany, he took on the job of writing my letters for me.

Then there was David Hamilton who had been at school with me. He had been in command of one of the anti-aircraft units at Maleme. Wounded in the foot, he had eventually been captured after he had tried to get away in a small boat. George Beale too used to come over and sit with me. We would relive the Battle of Crete, and discuss all the things that might have been done differently. And my Maleme doctor, Flying Officer Cullen, was also a regular visitor.

Boredom was our chief enemy. We were desperate in our attempts to defeat it. Every form of activity, mental or physical, was an escape from the monotony of existence. But we were running away from the real issues. The fact was that our philosophy was inadequate to deal with our changed circumstances.

We were like men who had just been demobilised and did not know what to do. We were men who had lost our jobs. We were men who had been retired. No activity or hobby could replace the drive and satisfaction of a vocation, or delay indefinitely the ultimate defeat of being bored. From time to time we would escape from ourselves for a few fleeting hours, but our recapture was only a matter of time. Monotony was not only tiresome, it was a menace to life itself.

IV

The prolonged starvation diet weakened everybody. Those who were fit found that they got tired quickly; those who were ill made slower progress than they should have; those who were very ill died. Symptoms of beri-beri, which is a deficiency disease, appeared; legs became weak and the joints swollen. And hunger has a psychological as well as a physical effect. Tempers became short; men became angry over trifles. A fight nearly developed one day because one man had been given a slightly smaller slice of bread than his neighbour for two successive meals. And there was a commotion because it was thought that we were being given less food in our ward than in the other wards.

The hospital staff were criticised fiercely and freely about trifles, and petty gossip centred around some of the patients who were less popular than others. Hunger is a crisis, like fear, which shows up the best and the worst in human nature. Under crisis, men behave as they really are. They are no longer concealed by the cloak of custom or the pretence of position. They are themselves.

In this maelstrom of clashing personalities, Padre Forrest played a great part. He had been wounded whilst serving with an Australian infantry battalion. His wound was in his back so that he had to lie on his face for weeks until it was healed. In spite of the pain and inconvenience he never murmured or complained. He was considerate and appreciative to the order-

44

lies. He was cheerful too without being hearty. He was loved and admired by all. After he had recovered and was fit to move about again, he was retained in the hospital to act as the official chaplain.

For me, the days dragged past in endless procession. One day was very like the next. Only occasionally would there be any variation, as when we were raided by our own bombers. The sirens would sound and the lights would go out. We would listen intently for the first signs of approaching aircraft. The drone of engines would be heard far away as a few Wellingtons approached. Outside, the night would be stabbed by searchlights and red tracers would chase each other towards the stars. The noise of engines would grow closer till they passed overhead. Then there would be the whistle of descending bombs and the crash of heavy explosions. Gradually the welcome note of Bristol engines would fade into the distance. Only the glow of fires would sometimes remain and the occasional explosion of a delayed-action bomb in the distance.

These were moving occasions. I would wonder which of my friends was passing overhead, only a few thousand feet away. In my mind's eye I would picture the scene from up there and the return trip to the canal zone only three or four hours distant. Then the lighted mess and familiar faces and Air Force chatter. I longed for it all and for some means of stepping on board a passing craft to join the crew. As the engines faded in the distance one would come back to earth and the dreary ward with the dismal Future grimacing round the corner.

The first night we were raided the guards had not expected it. All those who could walk hurried up on to the roof and cheered as the bombers went over. They were hitting the Piraeus and fires burned till the next morning. But the cheers were resented and the guards, after failing to discover the culprits, warned us that anyone appearing on the roof after dusk, or at any time when a raid was in progress, would be shot. On subsequent occasions a guard would be posted up there while a raid was on.

It was a strange experience being raided by our own aircraft. It was good for morale. Very few of us were frightened of being hit. Personally, I should have welcomed it at that time. We all welcomed the evidence of British air power, particularly after the critical time in Crete when we knew there were so few aircraft left.

Normally, however, night-time at Athens contained no thrills. Towards the end of the evening the guards would come round and check the roll. It would be checked again the next morning. Then the orderlies would come round tidying up the beds and administering medicines. I would get my shot of morphia or my sleeping draught. The lights would be put out at about ten o'clock. As soon as this happened the trouble would start.

Athens in summer is the happy hunting-ground for millions of bed bugs. Our hospital must have been their advanced training-ground. We had hundreds of thousands. They emerged in the darkness and vanished as soon as a light appeared. So it was difficult to trace them to their lairs. Hundreds used to live in the springs of the beds and between the cracks in the woodwork of the rooms. A common sight each day was some-one or other in the ward debugging his bed with a candle. As the springs were heated hundreds of bugs would make a bid for freedom. Amid cries of delight they would be pounced upon by eager hands and crushed to their doom. A splash of blood would be their only memorial.

The first event of the day was a bug hunt. Usually a few stragglers would be spotted on the ceiling or halfway up the wall on their way home after a successful night's raiding. Amid great excitement a broom handle would be procured and the chase would begin. The kill would be marked by a red spot on the wall or ceiling.

I was powerless to protect myself from these bugs and they tortured me. I could feel them crawling on me and could only lie still and be bitten. I was unable to move a finger to help myself. I would bear it as long as I could and then call out for an orderly. He would come along with a torch and track down a bug or two. Then I would be left in darkness, a prey once more to the hordes that remained. By this time my sleeping draught would take effect and I would relapse into unconsciousness.

Things reached such a pitch that I complained to the doctors and a thorough search was instituted round my bed. A good many bugs were found and destroyed but still they came. Eventually the trouble was traced to my splint where several hundred were found to be nesting. After these had been removed I had less trouble.

I was also troubled by itch in the scalp. Most of us had skin trouble, probably caused by the diet. But being unable to scratch was a terrible handicap. The itch was maddening and I could only try to alleviate it by rubbing my head on the pillow. Some nights it nearly drove me demented and the orderlies did not appreciate being called out to scratch someone's head. Yet, if they had known it, the itch was harder to bear than almost anything else. Frequent washing helped to keep the scalp healthy, and I was able to persuade people to do this for me to avoid being disturbed at nights.

V

In the corner of the ward away from me a little group used to gather together and talk in low voices with many a glance behind them to make sure they were neither overheard nor overlooked. They were the escapers.

The escapers had a big idea where most of the others lacked it. It gave them something immediate and practical to live for. They thought and talked of escaping. They had plans where others were creatures of impulse. Exercise took on a new significance when related to a plan for escape. Otherwise it was a dreary task of vaguely keeping fit. The afternoon was a time of opportunity to study ways out of the camp instead of just a time to be passed. There were routes to study, clothes and food to collect, things to be done which must be kept secret. Romance and adventure. The escaper was a spark of life in a dead world.

Roy Farran used to come and talk to me. He was a slightly built, enthusiastic, young cavalry officer, who had been wounded in the leg in Crete. He preserved an appropriate air of mystery about his plans. But he was pleased to find a kindred spirit because the escapers were hotly criticised by many if not most of the other prisoners. Their most common attack was to say that escaping was selfish. It could do no good to anyone except possibly the escaper. On the contrary, it was liable to bring reprisals on the rest of the camp. This was the "peace at any price" school.

Another disguise for the same thing was to say that it was not fair to the folks at home. The escaper might disappear and never be heard of again; at the least he would disappear for several months.

Then there were those who said it wâs no good trying to escape. No one was succeeding in getting away and it only brought trouble on the Greeks. The whole thing was impossible. You might be successful in getting outside the camp, but what then? There was all that sea to cross. And even if you reached a neutral country they would just lock you up again. Besides, the Greeks were starving and would be unfriendly. These were the "no-hopers". They were greatly assisted in their subtle propaganda by the "failures". Those who had tried and had been recaptured. Naturally they made the most of their difficulties.

For those who were thinking of escaping such talk had its effect. Many might have tried if they had not been discouraged in this way. Defeatist talk always strikes a chord in a doubting mind. But there were those who saw clearly that it was their duty to try. And they had decided to act. Besides, this was adventure; "safety-first" was a policy of defeat. Escape became the motive for living for these men.

I envied them their health. For me, there was no hope. I was a cripple and still wavering between life and death. The future too was hopeless. I should never be fit enough to make the attempt. Nevertheless, I encouraged them as much as I could, and spoke up in their defence when they were being attacked. Others supported me and the ward was divided into two sides, those who believed it to be right to try to escape, and those who thought it wrong. For us, to be a willing prisoner was treachery to our country and our cause. For them, expediency had overruled principle. It was an age-old issue.

Roy Farran was a treat to talk to. He was so enthusiastic. The huge wound in his thigh made him very lame, but this did not deter him. He could move, however slowly, and he intended to move to freedom. Every afternoon he studied the habits of the guards and the approaches to the camp. Every strand of wire was examined, every dip in the ground became familiar. In the end, he slipped under the fence in broad daylight and limped boldly away in full view of the sentries, whose attention was distracted by people talking to them at the critical moment. He was successful in his attempt and reached Egypt in time to take part in the desert campaign of 1942. Later, he distinguished himself as a parachutist. His escape was a notable contribution to the war effort in every way.

Sandy Thomas was less successful at this stage, although he escaped later from Salonika and reached Egypt, after many months of adventure, in the spring of 1942. He was very tall and a conspicuous figure. Somewhat rashly he tried the same tactics as Roy Farran. With a white pillow case slung over his shoulder containing his gear, he walked up to the wire and started to cut his way through it. The white pillow case stood out in the failing light and the diversions were inadequate to occupy the sentries completely.

They saw him and shot at him. Fortunately, he was not hit. The sentries ran up to him and started to treat him roughly. He knocked them down and a fight ensued. He was dragged off to the guard-room and treated with some violence. But he was undaunted and soon he was with us planning for another attempt.

Others made a break from another camp nearby in a dust-storm when visibility was very restricted. They got away, and a number reached Egypt safely. Then there was Tim, an Australian. He hung about for weeks with his escaping kit packed in his pockets, watching for an opportunity. The weeks went by and no chance occurred. Then one evening he slipped under the wire along a sewage trench which was just being dug and got clean away. He also was eventually successful in reaching safety.

I watched them go and envied them. For me, the prospects grew blacker as the days went by. My health too was precarious. One evening, in the gloaming, I had a peculiar sense of growing weakness. I was getting breathless too. Suddenly, I realised that the bed was getting wet under me. I called out and an orderly came up. He took one look at me and ran. The artery in my right arm had opened up again and was spouting blood. My ears were singing faintly and I felt strangely light-headed and peaceful.

They put on a tourniquet quickly and Major Brooke Moore came up to investigate. I remember him turning up my eyelids and saying something about "shock". It was getting dark and there was no light in the ward. They prepared to operate on me where I lay as I could not be moved. The position of my out-stretched left arm was such that I could not be carried through the narrow doors to the operating theatre without disturbing the fracture.

Norman Rose, a young surgeon from Sydney, hunted for a vein into which to inject the anaesthetic. My blood pressure was too low to use one in my arm, so he gave it to me in the foot. I hardly noticed the stab of the needle and was quickly unconscious. The scene was dramatic. Norman held a torch while Brooke Moore opened up my right arm near the armpit and tied the brachial artery there. The rest of the ward looked on with keen interest.

They had caught it just in time and I regained consciousness later that night, weak, but alive. I remained in a very low condition for some weeks after this. To add to my troubles, I developed dysentery and was unable to hold my food. I spent many hours doubled up with acute pains in the belly. Some thought that I would not live through it, but life remained with me however anxious I was to give it up. True, I wanted to be an escaper. I wanted to escape from life. Instead I was destined to escape to live.

IV

ATHENS — CONVALESCENCE

I

It was stiflingly hot one afternoon in August. I lay outstretched on my bed as usual, panting with the heat. A blast of hot air was coming into the ward through the window above me. Others, like myself, lay naked on their beds, silent and prostrated by the heat. Athens in summer was hotter than Cairo, or felt like it.

Butch came in. "I'm off," he said. It was some moments before I realised the significance of his remark. Once before the Germans had tried to move him away to Germany, but he had been retained, at the request of our doctors, to look after me. I had relied completely on Butch for everything. Now he was going. I wondered what would happen to me. I began to realise just how much I owed to him and how much of his time and trouble had been devoted to me.

The next day he was away to the other camp nearby, ready to be shipped on to Salonika and thence by train to Germany. The doctors arranged for orderlies to take his place. In some ways, Butch's departure resulted in a new lease of life for me. Life without his constant attention was so unpleasant that I determined to get well. From that moment, my physical condition started to improve.

A few days later I called for Jock Wilson. Jock was a stretcher-bearer in the Black Watch. He came from Dundee and had been in the regular army before the war. He was a character, and a very good nursing orderly. He had done my daily dressings for many weeks.

I told him that I wanted to sit up. By this time, my arm was in a different type of splint, strapped to my body. Major Pallandri, who was my doctor during this period, was confident that it would be all right. For the first time in three months I sat up in bed. It does not sound much, but for me it was a great event. My arm hurt and I was very uncomfortable, but it was a start. It was also an opportunity for the orderlies to lift me out of bed and change my mattress.

Getting rid of the blood-soaked, pus-impregnated, stinking mattress was a great advance, and made me much more comfortable. After that I used to sit in bed, propped up by pillows, for a short time every day. It was a change to see the ward for the first time from a different angle. Somehow it looked quite different. But it was a painful process. My left arm ached and my right arm hurt as the blood ran into it under increased pressure. My heart palpitated too under the increased strain of tightened muscles and the effort of pumping blood up to my head instead of along the level. I got tired very quickly and my cushions had to be readjusted at frequent intervals. Jock was patient and changed them round every few minutes.

Part of the trouble was that I was so thin that my hip bones had no protection when I sat on them. They bruised the skin even with a cushion to sit on. They were sharp and angular. I was a bag of bones and there was no flesh anywhere on me. My joints stuck out in ungainly bulges and the skin lay in folds round me. With my arms stuck out in their splints, I looked and felt like a scarecrow. My weight had gone down to about half normal.

Once I had decided to get well, however, it was not long before I made my first sortie from my bed. First I sat up; two orderlies helped me; very slowly my legs were manoeuvred round till they hung over the edge of the bed. All this was done taking great care not to shake or move my arms in their splints, as the slightest movement caused me pain. Quite a crowd gathered to see how I got on. It was a big moment. I had no idea whether my legs would take any weight or not.

The orderlies helped me to slide slowly forward till my feet touched the floor. The cold stone made me exclaim as it touched the soft skin on the soles of my feet. The blood was throbbing in my feet and the veins bulged till they hurt with the unaccustomed pressure. My feet were on the floor. Slowly Jock lifted me till I was upright, my legs braced back to take the strain. Slowly he relaxed his grip round my waist. I was standing for the first time in more than three months.

I felt light-headed and a little giddy and my breath was coming fast with the effort I was making. I was sweating and the hot afternoon air blew in through the window on me. Very carefully, inch by inch, I manœuvred myself round till I was facing my own bed. The one behind me was vacant. Jock took the strain again and I sat down on it while he and the others changed my mattress and sheets. Then the performance was repeated, and I sat down on my own bed. Some more manœuvring and I was lying down again, utterly exhausted, but thrilled to be so far on the road to recovery again. I slept.

The very next day I determined to walk. We went through the same performance to get me on my feet. With my legs braced back all my weight was taken on the bones and none on the leg muscles which were practically non-existent. With the orderlies in close attendance behind me, I took a short step forward, stiff-legged and careful not to bend the knees, which would instantly have collapsed. It worked. I was unsteady but upright; that was all that mattered. The others looked on, amazed, as a tall skeleton tottered five paces down the ward, turned round with great difficulty and tottered back again. I was laid carefully down again, exhausted but triumphant.

The following day, I walked the length of the ward and back. Stark naked, I was an extraordinary sight with every rib standing out and folds of loose skin hanging on my bones. The knee joints stood out from my legs like balloons and there was no sign of muscle to be seen. The outstretched left arm in its splint and the right arm, ungainly in its full plaster, added to the incongruity of my appearance. Major Pallandri had a

54

camera; he took pictures of me as I staggered about, stiff-legged, but mobile once more.

I set myself the task of reaching the roof, which was up a flight of twenty steps. On my first attempt I could only get up one with help. The next day I managed six. The third day I reached the roof. It was a great moment. The orderlies had placed a bed there so that I could lie and rest before I came down.

I shall never forget coming out into the fresh sunshine that afternoon. The sun shone on me, it was warm and caressing. The air was faintly scented with the smell of wild herbs from the hills close by. It was my first glimpse of the world outside for three months. And what a world it was! To the west, as I emerged on to the roof, lay a range of hills close by. We were halfway up the slopes. To the south, the hills swept round to the coast and the Piraeus lay there, its streets and houses clustered round the harbour. To the east, the sparkling blue Aegean stretched away to the islands and the horizon. Small boats with white sails flitted about the bay which curved majestically to Athens and beyond. And there, to the north, laid out below us, the capital spread itself round the Acropolis as a cluster surrounds its jewel.

The matchless proportions of the Parthenon were clearly visible from where I stood. My eyes filled with tears at the exquisite beauty of the scene. Away behind, wooded slopes rose to a range of blue mountains and a valley ran towards Kifisia in the dove-grey distance. It was so lovely that I was overcome with emotion. I had not shed a tear through months of pain and moments of sharp agony; but this was too much. I lay on the bed and wept. It was partly the effect of the scene and partly the sense of achievement. I was recovering. For the first time in many weeks, life began to look worth living again.

II

From that day, early in September 1941, I made rapid progress. Within a few days, I was able to make the long journey down three flights of stairs and up another two to the X-ray room. The pictures showed that some union had occurred in my left shoulder, and my right forearm was forming new bone quite quickly. There was still extensive infection in both my wounds, however, and they continued to discharge freely.

With my arms trussed up, I was a strange figure. I had to go through all the doors sideways and I was unable to wear a coat or shirt. Some trousers had been procured for me, and also some canvas shoes of which I had to have the toes cut off to get my feet in. Apart from these I was naked. In the warm weather it was comfortable to go about like this, but as the weeks went by it became necessary to wear more clothes. So the hospital tailor made a cloak for me out of an old blanket. It had slits cut in it for my head and arms to stick through, and it was tied round me with tapes. But it was still a draughty garment.

Every day I used to clamber up the stairs to the roof and sit there. To start with, I could not endure more than ten to fifteen minutes of sunshine. Later I was able to stay up for nearly an hour at a time. I never tired of the exquisite view which had so overwhelmed me at first sight. Every day was the same, yet different. On the roof, one was in touch with the great world outside. Stray sights and sounds were the variables in the complex formula of life.

Processions of Greek civilians used to pass by, wending their laborious way up the hillside to collect wood for fuel. Some would have lean donkeys which would totter back under an enormous load. But mostly they were women and children dressed in rags. They could be seen high up on the hill gathering the wood, cutting down young shrubs and hacking away at the scrub oak and the thorn bushes which still covered the higher slopes. The main face of the hill was already bare of timber.

Away in the distance could be distinguished the faint noises of the city, the occasional hum of an army truck or the clatter of a train with their associated hoots or whistles. Now and again, parties of German soldiers could be heard, singing as they marched along with the measured pauses characteristic of their race. One, two three, sing! Pause! One, two, three, sing! The beat of the music was the beat of marching men, treading down the liberties of nations.

Then there were other songs; the songs of sad processions, each with a body, bound for the cemetery. They passed the hospital regularly. The bodies were sometimes in white coffins piled high with flowers in a horse-drawn hearse. Usually, however, they were carried by hand; and usually the bodies were just wrapped in cloth and carried on boards. The people were too poor for ceremony though never too poor to suffer and to weep. The pathetic processions were all too frequent. Young and old alike were perishing under the hardships of the occupation. We heard of men, women and children collapsing of starvation in the streets.

The hospital roof was an unsurpassed point of vantage. It was also a little world in itself. We were all types, halt and lame, sick and crippled, blind men, deaf men, as well as men with nothing worse than a flesh wound or a bout of dysentery or malaria. Immediately below us was the space surrounding the hospital, beyond was the wire with sentries at the corners. The "exercisers" used to parade round and round the building. It was six complete circuits to the mile. Some used to count the number of times round, others walked by the clock. At this stage, it was all that I could do to totter back and forwards a few times on the roof. I kept company with the men on crutches.

As time went by, the number of convalescents grew and the day came when enough had accumulated to justify shipping them north towards Germany. Men who were fit enough to travel in a hospital-ship and train but who had some permanent or lasting disability became eligible, under the Geneva Convention, for repatriation. A provisional repatriation list had been agreed with the German doctors. I was on this list, but was one of the last to be fit enough to move.

It was a memorable occasion when the first repatriates left for their long journey, long in time as well as distance because of hitches in the arrangements for repatriation. But at the time we thought it would be just a matter of weeks before these lucky cripples would be home. There was great excitement to see who would be on the list. When it was published there were many heart-burnings. We loaded the lucky ones with messages for our families.

The hospital ship was Italian, and it lay in the Piraeus in full view from the roof of the hospital. It was painted white with red crosses and was ringed with lights at night-time. I was still in bed when the boys left. I was excited and yet moved to see them leave. Blair Hughes-Stanton came to say goodbye. He promised to give all my news to my family. The party left the ward with a host of followers carrying their few belongings. The next day the ship had gone.

Many blank spaces were left in the wards, and we were reshuffled to make the best use of the space and staff available. I found myself in the next bed to a Captain Lionel Massey. Lionel was a young infantry officer who had been badly wounded in both legs, and he and I were the last two in the officers' ward to recover. His leg injuries were a great handicap to his mobility, and I quickly learned to walk faster than he could. On the other hand, his general condition was better than mine and he lasted longer, and was able to sit for long periods while I had to lie down.

Lionel was a Canadian, his father was High Commissioner for Canada in London. He had been educated at Oxford and I found him a delightful companion, interested in men and affairs. He was a keen art critic and used to be consulted widely by the various amateur and professional artists in the camp. His men too were devoted to him, and he had always visitors round him from some part of the hospital. So we were kept well-informed of the news.

One day they brought us news that a New Zealand sergeant, who was a patient in the hospital, had been awarded the Victoria Cross. The news had come through Geneva. The whole hospital rejoiced with him in this high honour, and he came round to our ward so that we could congratulate him.

His name was Sergeant Hinton.

Major Brooke Moore had told the German guard commander the news and had explained that this was the highest award for gallantry that the King could bestow. The Nazi-trained mind reflected on this, evidently wondering what the party line should be on such an occasion. Gallantry was of course a virtue held in high esteem. Perhaps it would be good for the party if . . .

Sergeant Hinton was sent for. When he heard that he was to report immediately to the orderly room he wondered for what crime he was being summoned. When he saw the whole German guard lined up outside the office he feared the worst. To his amazement, however, the corporal stepped forward and the whole guard saluted him. Ushered into the office with great ceremony, he was in a dream, wondering when he would wake up.

He found Major Brooke Moore laughing heartily at the irony of the position. It was indeed ironical that a man should be congratulated by his enemies for killing them. Yet it was an interesting point too. The Nazi régime depended for its success and for its very existence on the identification of noble virtues with its way of life. You had to compensate for concentration camps by their opposites. Courage was a virtue in any language and a good Nazi must honour it, even in his enemies, or reject a principle on which his way of life depended. Besides, it would help to win the British over to their way of thinking. Hence the little demonstration. It was a small thing, but significant.

I began to see the technique by which any dictatorship operates to retain the faith and allegiance of the millions. On the one hand, by the ruthless suppression and extermination of its enemies, allied with propaganda intended to identify them with every vice and every misfortune. On the other hand, by the encouragement of its friends by every means, promises and bribes, and the identification of the ruling régime with every virtue and with every success.

In this way, the ordinary people, reluctant to face persecution for their principles, readily rationalise away their qualms and quieten their consciences. It is always so much more satisfactory to blame someone else than to accept personal responsibility for mistakes. And when the popular theme is to blame a certain race or class for everything, people fall easy victims to the disease of "stigmitis" — the branding of the few with the infamy of many. The disease was not only a modern one in Nazi Germany and in other countries, but was identical with that which produced Calvary.

From this point, people proceed by easy stages to the point where they refuse to notice or think about the concentration camps in their midst, and are horrified when these are exposed. It is a sobering thought that, when men stop fighting for Christian principle, they become blind to the real moral issues in the world around them. They are ready to accept materialist solutions to moral problems, and this eventually leads them to slavery. They are promised efficiency in return for control, and sacrifice their freedom bit by bit until they are puppets who have no further say in how the community should be run.

I saw later that this trend towards the extremes of right and left was still a danger to the democracies which victory over Nazism and Fascism would not eliminate. We could eventually fall victims to dictatorship ourselves. What we needed was the moral and spiritual conviction to make people cooperate of their own free will to make society more effective, as well as more attractive, than the dictatorships of either right or left. William Penn's dictum, "Men must choose to be governed by God or they condemn themselves to be ruled by tyrants" has never been more true or timely.

III

About this time we were told that all R.A.F. prisoners were going to be flown to Germany in a Junkers 52. There were about a dozen of us left to whom this could apply. I gathered the others round me and we hatched a plot. A number of the airmen were in the convalescent stage including Sergeant Alec Butterick, one of my pilots who had lost a leg. The plan was to seize the aircraft while in flight and fly it to Turkey. I could work the rudder with my comparatively effective legs while Alec Butterick would handle the other controls as advised by me. The seizure of the aircraft was planned on the assumption that there would be the normal crew of three plus one armed escort.

We were to wait until we had taken off and settled down at a reasonable height on course for Germany. Then, on a given signal from me, each airman was detailed for a job. Two would simultaneously attack the escort, taking him by surprise. At the same time others were to knock out the crew. The plan would depend for its success on co-ordination and surprise. Alec and I were to crawl forward as quickly as possible and take over the controls from the unconscious pilot. The men rehearsed their parts in imagination, and we were all keyed up for the adventure. But, possibly due to careless talk among the men, the arrangements for us to be flown were suddenly cancelled without any reason being given. We were bitterly disappointed.

The monotony of prison hospital was unbroken for a time. Boredom and self-pity bound us all in unseen but none the less effective chains. After a good deal of agitation by the doctors, on the grounds of health, parties of convalescent patients were allowed to proceed with a percentage of the medical staff under escort for walks outside the camp. They were all required to give their parole not to try to escape, in spite of the provision of an armed escort. This raised the thorny question of the propriety of giving your parole to the enemy. Some held it to be sensible and therefore right. Others maintained that it was quite wrong. They were usually people who were unable to go anyway. Others took the view that it was permissible provided it did not compromise one's chances of escape at some other time. As the parole was withdrawn when each walk was over, the majority took this latter view.

The walks broke the monotony for many besides those who were able to take part in them. I was unable to go out, but greatly enjoyed the descriptions of life outside from the lucky ones who had been there. It was not long before the walks became an excuse to take the guards into a local wine shop and make them drunk. Soon the parties of walkers used to return to hospital carrying all sorts of forbidden imports, such as bottles of Greek wine, occasional sausages which were of very doubtful origin, and additional fruit.

They all spoke warmly of the Greek people in the streets who were quite unafraid to show their sympathy and friendship for us in full view of the German guards. They would press gifts of fruit and cigarettes on our men and even, on occasions, bread which by then was almost unobtainable for large numbers of the civil population. The conditions became increasingly bad outside and men, women and children were reported to be starving in the streets of Athens. Eventually the walks were curtailed and only the medical staff were allowed outside for strictly supervised exercise.

One day, months after I had been admitted to hospital, there was a commotion throughout the camp. Word went round that we were at last to be interrogated by German intelligence officers. The interrogation of the whole camp was done in two days. The men had all their papers confiscated for examination. Weeks later they were returned. I had no papers except a few scrap notes of the home addresses of fellow patients in the hospital in case I should return home before them. I was ill in bed. A German officer of the Luftwaffe examined the R.A.F. prisoners. He arrived at my bed accompanied by two N.C.O.s. He spoke very good English and asked what was the matter with me. I told him where I was wounded. He sympathised and asked if I had any papers. I did not reply and he glanced at the table beside my bed and picked up my addresses. He told me he would have to take them as a matter of formality, but that they would be returned to me as soon as possible. They came back about two weeks later. I discovered from the men that his name was Henkel and he used to play tennis for Germany at Wimbledon. He departed with a courteous farewell, saying that he hoped I would soon be well again.

As the patients recovered in health, activities became more and more organised and active. The Australians used to play endless "two-up" games. The game of two-up is a complicated version of heads and tails. You toss two coins at once and bet on the result. There is a ring master who shouts the odds, and the afternoon used to be punctuated by raucous cries of "I want a hundred" from the ring master laying off his bets. A good deal of money used to change hands at these games. One friend of mine made the equivalent of a hundred pounds sterling one afternoon and lost it and more during the evening.

As I became more active I used to go and visit some of my airmen in other wards through the hospital. One in particular was very badly wounded and had been hovering between life and death for many months. His name was Albert Moore and he had been wounded with bomb splinters in Crete. He had more than sixty wounds on him and his belly and back were lacerated and torn with shrapnel. A deep stomach wound gave him great pain and discomfort and another splinter in the bone of his pelvis had produced a lasting infection of the bone there. Yet with it all he was one of the most cheerful men in the place. He always had a smile for every visitor and his patience and courage were an inspiration to many. He wasted away to a skeleton, but his will to live was undiminished, and he fought through to partial recovery before I left him. He was later repatriated.

By November 1941, most of the wounded had recovered sufficiently to be moved on to Germany. The last big batch of men numbered about three hundred and included most of my friends. I was left with about eighty others as the final dregs of the hospital. There was one other officer who had been in another ward and whom I had not met. I was walking much more strongly by now, but I was still too weak to sit for long periods. The question arose how to attend to me in view of the greatly reduced numbers of men available. I was still unable to use either arm and so had to have everything done for me, from washing my teeth to smoking a cigarette. I was moved to a small room by myself near the doctors' quarters and six of my own men undertook to look after me.

They had to start off, first thing in the morning, with washing and shaving me. Then they would feed me with my breakfast and sit with me to hold a cigarette or to brush off the flies as required. When I got up, I would have to be dressed in my trousers and shoes and cloak. Then perhaps I would dismiss whoever was with me at the time for an hour or so while I took my exercise and did my round of visits to the lads who were in bed. Then there was lunch to give me and pillows to arrange on my bed to support my arms when I lay down or sat up. Then the evening meal to feed to me. And countless odd jobs in between.

In the evening, the doctors used to cook themselves something from their Red Cross parcels. We used to pool our resources and have some tasty dish each day as a result. I joined them and they would help me to eat. Then it would be time for bed and one of my lads would be there to help me to settle in for the night. My weakness and inability to do the smallest thing for myself were exceedingly irksome to me as well as to others. They were a continual source of irritation and depression. I put on a mask of cheerfulness which I did not feel. The mask frequently slipped off and revealed the miserable frustrated soul below.

IV

By this time, the doctors who had seen me through my most difficult days had been sent on to Germany. The medical staff had been reduced to the minimum required to look after the residue of about eighty wounded. Half a dozen doctors were left, including Major Brooke Moore who had been in charge all through. It was my first real opportunity to get to know them and during these last weeks in Athens I began to see and appreciate the tremendous task they had accomplished there.

Apart from the large numbers of sick and wounded men who

had been successfully treated in the hospital under very difficult circumstances and with a relatively low death rate, one of the most striking tributes to their work was the surprisingly low incidence of neurosis. We had very few "nerve cases" in spite of conditions which were unusually favourable for producing them. Nervous breakdown was rare and the morale of the hospital was high in spite of many demoralising influences. There were, of course, incidents and things did not always run smoothly, but it was a noteworthy achievement that more trouble was not experienced. Men were shaken by the past, pained and wearied by the present, in dread of the future, but still unbroken. It was at once a tribute to the quality of the staff and to the basic spirit latent in the British race and tradition.

Padre Forrest played a big part in this achievement. Not by preaching sermons, although he did this well, but by being a living example of a man with an answer to his own problems. He was invariably cheerful, not hearty, but in a quiet way, and he was peaceful. The hospital was full of men who wanted that quality for themselves. They were depressed or falsely hearty. They were resigned rather than patient, they were hungry for good news, they longed to be free, not only from prison but also from problems.

The padre used to come and sit by my bed and we would talk. I told him all about my home and family and my connection with the Church. I also told him that I did not believe in God, although I condescendingly approved of Christian ethics. He would smile and tell me about his home and parish in Australia, or his days with an infantry battalion. He would never argue metaphysics with me however hard I tried to involve him; instead he gave me a pocket New Testament. Although I did not read it then, it was to play a big part later.

Everybody in the hospital liked the padre, and his Sunday services were crowded out. The old familiar hymns were a link with happier days, and his brief sermons were practical advice from his own experience. His prayers too were simple and moving and sincere. There is no doubt that he helped many to retain their balance through these precarious days.

The doctors too were an unconscious influence in preserving morale. They maintained a cheerful air and organised diversionary activity of every sort to help to keep the men from thinking too much about themselves. The greatest occasion in the history of the hospital was the sports meeting held one Saturday in the autumn.

It was preceded by several weeks of intense activity. Every ward had its candidates for the different events. The teams went into training and practised arduously. The bookmakers did a lively trade. Each "stable" had its "favourites" and "hot tips" were whispered around. Much money was laid and the odds were kept posted up all over the hospital.

As the day got nearer, excitement grew and the different "stables" became secretive about their favourites. It was difficult to enter the wards to visit friends. The doors were kept shut and visitors were scrutinised before being allowed to enter in case they were "bookie's touts" studying form. Everybody read the news-sheet which was typed and circulated giving the latest news from each "stable". The whole hospital was racing mad. It was a great game and one which mystified the Germans. They were suspicious and evidently suspected that we were brewing up some trouble or other. They became more vigilant and careful with their daily checks.

Early in the morning on the day of the races, men were astir. The bookies were working out their starting prices. Stewards were outside preparing the course. The newspaper men were typing their "eve of the race" news. The big event was the Melbourne Cup, the Australian Derby. The course was about fifty yards long and the event consisted of running one way with the "jockey" up and the other with the "mount" up. The favourite was one of the doctors with another doctor as his jockey. A burly pair of medical orderlies were also strongly fancied.

By midday the excitement was intense. The races were the sole topic of conversation. Every patient, fit to be moved, was helped outside into the sunshine. Beds were carried out and placed in a shady viewpoint which was the grandstand. The crowd were excited with the irresponsible gaiety characteristic of all race meetings. Bookies were shouting the odds and everyone hastened to place money on their choice.

At two o'clock the races began. The first was a long distance event in which the contestants had to walk right round the hospital. Major Brooke Moore was fancied by many on account of his long legs. There was a large field of about twenty starters. The shout went up, "They're off!" Loud laughter greeted them as they fought for position on the corner. A walking race is always an ungainly affair and this was no exception. They disappeared behind the hospital. A howl from the nether regions announced that Major Brooke Moore had broken into a trot and had been disqualified. The field was in sight again and everyone strained to see who was in the lead. The noise was terrific as they came round into the home straight. A lanky medical orderly swept in to win amid thunderous applause.

Queues formed up in front of the bookies as the winners hurried in to stake their claims. Soon, fresh odds were being given for the next race, the Melbourne Cup itself. Every window was crowded and there was a seething mob around the track as the starters lined up. The crowd was hilarious by now and wisecracks were flying. The jockeys mounted their steeds and moved precariously about on the starting line. A roar announced that they were off and tremendous excitement reigned as the field staggered up the course. Starving men are not strong in the legs and there were several falls. The change-over was accomplished amid much laughter and barracking and the jockeys carried their steeds back on the home straight. A great deal of money was about to change hands and the excitement rose to a climax. The winners fell across the finishing line and were mobbed by the ecstatic crowd. The bookies looked gloomy. The favourite had won.

The events went on all afternoon. There was a long jump. This produced some interesting medical data. Most of the entrants were drawn from the medical staff as few patients were in a fit condition to participate. The staff were all suffering from lack of food. Many were athletes of good repute who should have jumped eighteen feet easily. But the best was about twelve feet. This was an indication of how close most men were to having beri-beri, the deficiency disease whose first symptom is weakness of the leg muscles.

By the end of the afternoon, an exhausted but happy crowd had dispersed to their respective wards again. The races had been a great success for all except the bookies, who had gone bankrupt about halfway through the proceedings. For days afterwards there was happy reminiscence of the events. How Major Brooke Moore had run in the walking race and another member of the staff had walked in the running race. And how the guards had stood by with loaded guns, mystified at the scene.

Indeed, our enemies must have found us very difficult to comprehend. The complete absorption of the British in a sports meeting held behind the wire was hard to understand. Our happiness was inappropriate. Prisoners should be sad and humiliated. Our behaviour was inexplicable. Yet we were just happy children playing games. For that day at least we had won our battle to be free. We would go on fighting, wherever we were.

V

One day, late in November, orders were received that the hospital at Athens was to close down. All remaining patients and the staff were to be sent on to Salonika, en route for Germany. We had expected this for some time and it was welcome news. Any change to the monotony of our existence was welcome.

Our departure from Athens was not marked by any ceremony. We were herded together one morning with our blankets and whatever kit we possessed and loaded in ambulances and buses. A few of the staff were staying behind to tidy up. "Brookie" was staying to the end with them. We were cheerful as we drove away. It was partly derived from the excitement of change. The familiar scenes were being left behind and every corner concealed something new and strange. The bus bumped along the dusty road to the harbour.

There, we were herded across the gangway on to the hospital ship. It had been a steam yacht in happier days. Now it was fitted out to carry two or three hundred wounded. Half the crew were Germans and the rest Greeks. The Greeks made sympathetic gestures to us when the Germans were not looking. They made it clear that they did not feel kindly towards their temporary masters.

Down below we found our bunks, comfortable enough in the cramped quarters available. Outside the officers' cabin I noticed a rack of rifles. They were not padlocked and were complete with bolts. I made a quick mental note of their position.

We were allowed on deck again as we steamed out of the harbour. Away up on the hills behind, the hospital stood out white against the olive green slopes, shining in the sunshine. We stood, spellbound, as the ship moved out in the bay and the shore receded till the houses merged into the pattern of colour that was Athens. The sweep of the bay was behind us, the sparkling blue Aegean ahead. The warm sea air was salt to taste and brisk to breathe. We drew it into our lungs with deep appreciative breaths. We were on the move at last.

Our first meal on board was a banquet. We had meat and potatoes, and white bread. And we could buy a bottle of beer from the German canteen. We could talk of nothing but the wonder of that meal. The food was simple but good, and there was enough of it. To starving men the change was almost too good to be true.

We slept well. When we woke, we were steaming up the channel between the island of Euboea and the mainland. The mountains rose straight from the water in steep and rocky slopes. But for the sunshine and clear blue sky we might have been sailing up any loch on the west coast of Scotland.

I started to hatch a plan. I noticed that the German crew had their meals separately from the Greeks. It meant that they were all in one room at one time. The officers were the same. A few determined men could seize them and control the ship.

We were due to round the north of Euboea late that day if we did not stop anywhere on the way. From there the Turkish coast was only about 120 miles away. We could be there early the next morning. I was confident that the Greek crew would support us.

I put my proposals to the doctors, suggesting that we use some of our medical orderlies for the job. The rifles outside our cabin were a gift for the taking. But my scheme was firmly rejected on ethical grounds. It was argued that we were travelling on a Red Cross ship under the privileges accorded to the Red Cross by international agreement. It would be a violation of the Geneva Convention to seize the ship and direct it to neutral waters. It would have disastrous consequences for all our wounded in the future.

I argued that we were prisoners and therefore entitled to make our escape whatever the circumstances. We had given no parole or undertaking of any sort not to attempt to escape. But the others would not hear of it. In retrospect, it is clear that they were right. The Germans would certainly have accused us of contravening the Geneva Convention. Lawyers might possibly have argued our case, but the escape of a few prisoners was not justifiable if it was to compromise an international agreement. One reason Britain was at war was in protest at the breaking of such agreements by the enemy. So we sailed serenely on.

All through the next day we sailed in the sunshine across the Gulf of Salonika. A patrol of Me 109s came over us from the direction of Larissa. They flashed over, dark against the sky, and circled widely back to the mainland. Mount Olympus lay on the port beam, massive and snow-capped in the distance and surrounded by range upon range of mountains. The scene was superb.

Our arrival in Salonika was uneventful. We tied up along-side the quay and walked off. Lorries were waiting and we were closed in and driven off quickly. Each lorry was guarded by a soldier with a tommy-gun and there was no opportunity to make a break for freedom.

As we rumbled over the cobbled streets we were silent, each absorbed in his own thoughts, each eager to pierce the veil which concealed the future. I wondered how long it would take us to reach Germany; how soon I should be examined for repatriation, how long after that. . . . Home was the goal to which every thought eventually turned. It was the cradle of our dearest hopes. There, we should find satisfaction at last, happiness, freedom, the answer to every problem, the fulfilment of every desire. Or should we? We lived in a world of wishful dreams. Could they come true? That was the question which ultimately had to be answered.

V

SALONIKA — DULAG 183

I

The lorries jerked to a standstill. The door was opened by a British warrant officer. He pointed to some barrack blocks behind a high barbed-wire fence. This was to be our home till we went on to Germany. Anything less like a home could scarcely be imagined. It was the infamous Dulag 183.

The transit camp consisted of four blocks of buildings. It was about one hundred yards square, and was surrounded by a twelve-foot high double fence. The strands of barbed wire were only about six inches apart and there were also diagonal strands to contend with. In between the two fences was a space of about five yards heaped high with rolls of barbed wire. It would be a long job to cut a path through that obstacle. At opposite corners of the square were wooden towers commanding each lane of wire. Sentries stood there by day and night with machine-guns ready loaded. At night searchlights in the towers swung from one lane of wire to the other in turn, all through the hours of darkness. Escape would be much more difficult than at Athens.

We inspected our new quarters. After the comparative luxury of the hospital at Athens, the place appalled us. It had been built as a barracks for the Turks in the years of the Turkish occupation and the sanitary arrangements were extremely primitive. The buildings stank. The fuel shortage had resulted in every stick of furniture being used for firewood, and doors were also missing in many instances. Few of the windows remained intact and the dust and dirt everywhere was appalling.

Each barrack-room had one small stove but the fuel was only sufficient to light one fire in each building. The cookhouse was in a distant shed where the facilities were extremely limited. Fortunately, perhaps, we had little to cook. We gathered in a huddle around our stove and depression settled heavily on everyone.

Every able-bodied man was soon engaged busily on bed making. There were some old iron bedsteads, crawling with bugs, but better than the floor. Some old palliasses were issued to us from the prison store and we had our own blankets from the hospital at Athens. Meantime, the doctors were busy checking over their patients to see that they had withstood the journey all right. Before long, the cooks had produced a cup of tea from Red Cross parcels and also a soup or thin stew from the same source. Our spirits began to rise again.

Later, we sat and listened eagerly as the skeleton staff left behind to receive us retailed the previous history of the place. There were grim stories of starvation with many cases of beri-beri; fourteen men had died of it. Others had been shot while trying to escape or being suspected of trying; their bodies had been left hanging on the wire till morning. We heard too how the whole camp was riddled with tunnels in various stages of completion. Two of these had been finished but had been discovered and blocked up. Twenty-four thousand men had passed through the camp before us. Some of them had only stayed a few days; others had been there for months. Eventually all were despatched in railway trucks up the long single line railway to Belgrade and beyond to the camps in Poland, Silesia, and elsewhere.

The routine of the camp was similar to that at Athens. We had two parades a day to call the roll; able-bodied men had to go outside for this and form up in two ranks. The rest of us had to sit by our beds or in the wards while the Germans came round to check our names off on their lists. Then there was an inspection of the camp every morning by the Commandant. During it we had to be by our beds as he came round, accompanied by the two British warrant officers who had been there since the camp started and who spoke good German.

The warrant officers had an office in the administration block, outside the wire, and they were allowed out for walks in the town. Their job was to assist the guards as interpreters and to provide fatigue parties whenever labour was wanted such as for cleaning out the stables or shifting stores. They were on friendly terms with the guard and were therefore extremely unpopular among their fellow prisoners. Their defence was typical of collaborators the world over. They had compromised with principle and were blind to the moral issues at stake. They argued expediency as justification. It made conditions easier for all if they were cooperative and friendly with the Germans. Thus for men as for nations, where principle was sacrificed to expediency, they ceased to fight.

As at Athens, the power behind the scenes was the SS man, the "Gefreiter" in charge of the guard. It was he who made life difficult for us with petty rules and regulations. The Commandant seemed to have no power over him. He himself was spied upon by the Gestapo. The Commandant was called Hauptman Severin. He was a middle-aged farmer from Westphalia. He was a kindly enough man who wanted as little trouble as possible. He used to inspect every room punctiliously and inquire for the health of our worst cases. He undertook to make representation to his headquarters about our living conditions and especially about the diet. But nothing came of it. His main interest was in his farm, and he would talk farming endlessly if given the opportunity.

Dick Mann and I shared a room together. He was the only other wounded officer. Dick had been in a different ward from me at Athens so I had not really known him before except through casual meetings. Now we were thrown together and became close friends. He had a sheep station in Australia and the Commandant used to come and talk sheep to him through an interpreter. He grew genuinely attached to Dick and used to smuggle in special delicacies for him when he was very ill.

Dick was a lieutenant in the Australian infantry. He had won the Military Cross at Bardia where his battalion had led the assault and he had been wounded in the chest by machine-gun fire as he led his platoon in to the attack. He was a big fellow, tall and well-built with brown hair and an engaging smile; his men thought much of him. After the desert campaign they had come to Greece and had fought their way through that tragic retreat with great distinction.

In Crete, they had fought at Retimo and pushed back the assault of the German paratroops for a time. Finally they had been outflanked and outnumbered. Dick was leading his men in a desperate counter-attack when he was hit by machine-gun fire in the legs. With one femur shattered he lay out until he was picked up by the Germans. For long months he lay at Athens fighting for life. He was too weak to stand an amputation and his festering leg kept him hovering on the brink between life and death.

Now it seemed as if he was recovering. He was able to get about on crutches for a time. But the conditions at Salonika were too bad. He had a relapse and his leg flared up and quickly reduced him to a bag of bones again. He suffered terrible pain with it too. We became very close to each other in the fellowship of suffering.

II

Our doctors were a young and lively gang. They were from Sydney and had been together all the time. Outstanding among them was David Leake, who had looked after Dick Mann all through these difficult months. He was one of those rare doctors whose interest in their patients is more than professional. He was a philosopher and friend to them as well. The others were delightful also and were extremely good to me personally. They took endless pains to help me use my arms again. They were a great team. They worked together and their results were correspondingly successful. It was vitally important that we should have really first-class medical attention at Salonika where, otherwise, conditions were so bad. Many owed their lives to the unstinting care of these doctors and their medical orderlies.

We used to sit together round the stove. Food would be brought in. A thin stew or soup made of beans and water, with our very small meat ration in it. I was made to feed myself. It was an exasperating business and I would much rather have allowed one of my men to do it for me. But then I should never have learned to use my arms again. So I was forced to do it or starve. Painfully, I would strain to reach my mouth with my left hand, the spoon spilling all the time so that when it reached my mouth there was practically nothing left to eat. Mercilessly, Norman or Vernon or Mackie would goad me on with taunts or threats. One day they made me carry the coffee jug so that it stretched my right arm. It was agonising but essential. The bent arm would have to come straight in time and the sooner the better.

Another day they decided to operate on me to straighten the arm and also manipulate some of the fingers on my right hand which were doubled up and useless. It was bitterly cold as I lay on a bed in an empty room. They prepared to operate, but had difficulty in finding a vein big enough for the anaesthetic injection. My blood pressure was low and the cold did not help matters. Eventually a vein in my foot was induced by pressure to swell enough to get the needle in and I passed quickly out under the influence of the "Evipan".

This type of anaesthetic has an intoxicating effect and, when the patient wakes, he frequently exhibits the symptoms of drunkenness. I woke in an empty room. I felt very cheerful. So I staggered to my feet and lurched to the door humming a little tune. I had difficulty in keeping a straight course and found this intensely amusing. I roared with laughter and bounced off the passage walls. Soon I was outside in the open. I headed unsteadily for the barbed wire. Reaching it, I became aware that men were marching up and down on the other side.

This was not unusual, as the Germans used the barrack square on the other side of the wire for drilling. They would spend hours goose-stepping and practising infantry drill. I saw these squads of men parading up and down. They were not drilling properly. In my best parade ground bellow I shouted "Halt". The effect was gratifying. Numbers of men halted abruptly. The German word of command was practically the same. "About turn" I bellowed. This was not so well received. The guards were realising that something was wrong and machine-guns were being trained in my direction. Men rushed up to me and hustled me, protesting loudly, inside the nearest building, as others explained hurriedly to the guards that I was under the influence of an anaesthetic.

By the time the Commandant arrived, I was singing at the top of my voice and I greeted him uproariously. He was taken aback and, having satisfied himself that I was indeed anaesthetised, he disappeared to smooth down the ruffled feelings of the local garrison. The doctors were delighted and my behaviour was a source of comment and amusement for a considerable time. I knew little of what I had done and was snoring peacefully in my bed again.

The weather became rapidly colder. Soon we were living in severe winter conditions with the temperature well below zero. Snow lay deep on the ground and everything was frozen hard. We battled to keep warm with great difficulty. One stove in each barrack block was kept going all day. We had just enough fuel to do this. Everyone huddled round the stove or stayed in bed. I stayed in bed with all my clothes on, and still I was cold.

Exercise was one way of getting warm. We used to pace up and down the wire. Sometimes we aped the German custom of singing with precise and measured pauses. The guards were never sure whether we were making fun of them or not.

Some of the orderlies were extremely hardy. There was a hose in an open shed which somehow had not frozen up yet. They used to strip naked in the snow and hose each other down with icy water. It was extreme but it kept the circulation working overtime and they claimed to be immune to the cold. Later the pipe froze and the custom was abandoned.

The cold weather produced other effects. There were always a good number of sewer rats about. But the cold spell made them bold and they were to be seen everywhere on the prowl. They were huge, hideous creatures. They came from the sewers through the indescribable filth of the Turkish lavatories. As you entered the dark and stinking place there would be a scurry of rats round the corner. As they got bolder, they would come up the drains while you were there. A hideous fanged face would appear over the edge of the drain. A long, bloated body would follow and the beast would pad away on the ice, its long tail disappearing round the door. The rats were as big as cats and a cat would have a rough time in a fight with them. At night you could hear them squeal as they fought each other.

We lived from day to day in hopeless squalor. It was too cold to wash or change clothes or do anything except stay in bed. Dick and I would lie silent for hours, shivering as the darkness deepened in the evening. There was nothing to say or do. We just lay. The draughts whistled round the ill-fitting door and through the broken window. The dust and dirt were thick on the floor and we were oppressed and hopeless.

III

After we had been in the camp a few weeks, Brooke Moore and the remainder of the staff arrived in from Athens. They had closed the hospital there and handed it over to the Germans who were going to use it as a hospital for their own wounded. They were only with us a week or so before they were moved on to Germany. It was good to see the padre again. He was in great spirits, and it cheered us up to have him around. The cold weather was no match for the warmth of his heart.

When they were told that they were to leave for Germany, we were surprised as we thought we should all go on together. But the snow, aided by constant sabotage by Greek patriots, kept the single line railway to Belgrade impassable for hospital trains. Ordinary trains had to stop and passengers had to walk some distance and get into another train on the other side of a river where the bridge had been blown up. The hospital staff headed by Brooke Moore were to travel in this way, but we, with our four doctors and few orderlies, were to await a hospital train.

So we said good-bye to them again. Before they left, the padre approached me and asked if I would do him a favour. I said "Of course" and asked what it was. He said: "You are the senior officer here now, and I wanted to make sure that the men have a service on Christmas Day." I was relieved to find he wanted to arrange something as simple as this, and said that I should certainly arrange for this to be done. But the padre was not satisfied. He said, "I want you to take it yourself." I was horrified at the prospect and quickly remonstrated with him, pointing out that, as he knew, I did not believe in these things. But he smilingly insisted that he had a special reason for asking me, so I agreed. After all, he had been very decent to me personally, writing my letters home and coming to talk to me when I was lonely. Why not? It would do no harm. No one need be offended.

As Christmas Day approached, I began to wonder what I should say to these men. I toyed with the idea of having a service with hymns and prayers and the old carols and leaving it at that. But something told me that I should have to speak as well. I did not relish the prospect.

In the meantime, great preparations were going on to make the day into a festival. We saved up a week's meat ration so that each man could actually have a piece of meat. Decorations were being devised with great ingenuity. The Commandant let us import some Greek wine for the occasion. By this time too America had entered the war and an American couple called House had joined us in captivity. There were also various Greeks with American nationality and some Greek officers, so we had quite an international gathering.

79

Charles House and his wife were an outstanding couple. His father had come to the Balkans in 1870 to do missionary work. As a development of it, he had founded a school near Salonika to teach the wild Greek mountaineers modern farming and village crafts. The school was renowned throughout the Balkans and had done much to improve the conditions of living in northern Greece. Charles had taken it over from his father after the last war, when the original buildings had been destroyed, and together they had rebuilt it and carried on with the expanding work. The Houses occupied a unique place in the affections of these wild mountain people and probably knew more of Balkan politics and troubles than any other authorities.

To us in prison, they were a constant source of encouragement and practical help. They were able to lay hands on precious things like fresh milk and even eggs for our worst cases. Many, including Dick Mann, owed their lives to these vital supplies of proper food at critical times. They were also able to supply many of the men with cigarettes which, at the time, were hard to obtain. They always had friends outside who had what was needed, whether it was books or clothes or supplies of this or that necessity. Their interest in people was such that each man in the ward felt they had come to visit him personally, and their influence on morale in this way was none the less powerful for being impossible to assess. They were destined to play a big part in my future.

Christmas Day dawned seasonably with a fresh fall of snow. It was bitterly cold. But inside the long barrack-room, which was our main ward, it was unusually cosy and cheerful. All three stoves were going and everyone crowded in to sit on the beds or on chairs beside our badly wounded men. Dick and I made our way there across the snow together. It was Dick's last appearance on crutches for many months, as he had a severe relapse afterwards.

I had just finished reading up the Christmas story in my pocket New Testament, and was thinking hard what I could say about it. We found that someone had procured an old pedal harmonium for the occasion and there was one of my airmen who knew all the tunes. So we had a good start. The men all had copies of the Australian Army Prayer Book which had some of the carols and old favourite hymns in it. We started off by singing. The old tunes had associations with home for all of us, and there was something timeless and moving about them. We read the formal prayers prescribed. Then it was time for me to speak.

I said that it was a strange Christmas for us behind barbed wire, but it was still the anniversary of a remarkable event. Nearly two thousand years ago, Jesus Christ had been born. Whatever might be our views, I added cautiously, we had to admit that His life and teaching had exerted a remarkable influence on world history. If only people would follow His example and live as He had lived, we should not have to fight bloody wars or see our comrades wasting away the years in unemployment between the wars. After this war, there would be much for us to do. We could not do better than live as Jesus had taught and make sure that the world was run on Christian principles.

My address was short and to the point. What was more, I had said nothing that I did not sincerely believe. We carried on with a hymn or two and ended by singing "Holy Night". The lovely lilting cadences, sung with great feeling by more than a hundred men, filled the air. Many of us were deeply moved. As we began the second verse, our voices were joined melodiously from outside the building — tenor, baritone and bass chanting in perfect harmony with us — it was the German guards singing "Heilige Nacht". In a foul prison camp, far from home, enemies were reconciled for a moment in mutual homage to the Son of Mary. A fragment from the past? An omen for the future?

After the service, many came up to me and said how much they had appreciated what I had said. David Leake told me that I had mistaken my profession. He said that it was my

81

sincerity which had gripped and impressed him. Charles House came up and added his thanks, saying that it had been an inspiration and help to him and his wife. This tribute, more than any other, astounded me. I had no idea that people appreciated the sort of talk I had given them. I felt extremely shamefaced. Of all people, what right had I to talk? I, who for years had denied the existence of God and who had always acted for my own interests.

But Christmas Day was a great success. For one day at least we were determined to celebrate. Our celebrations took the usual form. We ate and drank. The food was a special treat and we had our first square meal since coming up on the hospital ship. There was roast meat of sorts, probably horse. And a roast potato each. And a Christmas pudding concocted from Red Cross parcels donated for the occasion from the store. And there was lots of sweet Samos and ordinary red wine. We drank and became merry. We sang and slept.

The next day, everything was back to normal again, including our tempers. Depressed and irritated with each other, we rubbed along as best we could. And from that time many began to relapse in health. It was partly the prolonged cold weather and partly the starvation diet and living conditions generally. One of our worst cases, who had a disarticulated leg, was removed to a German hospital nearby. He developed jaundice and died.

I was included on the funeral party on account of my newly won reputation as a conductor of religious services! We got aboard a lorry with the usual armed escort and drove off to the hospital. There, the coffin was taken on. The lorry skidded and bumped on the snow-covered roads and we climbed a hill up to the war cemetery where thousands of casualties of the last war lie in neat rows of white crosses. A grave had been prepared and we slow-marched with the coffin through cypress-lined avenues to the graveside. It was bitterly cold, our breath steamed in front of us and icicles formed in our hair.

But it was a lovely scene with the snow-covered ground and

trees laden with white. We laid him down and I read a short burial service from my Army Prayer Book. The coffin was draped with the Union Jack and German soldiers fired a salute over it. We left him in that quiet spot on the hill surrounded by his comrades. Soon, the place would be just another cross on a hillside — one more milestone on the road to freedom.

IV

The cold weather persisted, and I continued to spend most of the time in bed with all my clothes on. It was a constant battle day and night to keep warm. From time to time we were joined by a fresh batch of prisoners on their way through to Germany. Usually they did not stay long, perhaps a few days, and then they would march away again. In one of these batches there was a young Australian sergeant-pilot. He was the first Air Force prisoner to go through who had not been with us in Crete.

His name was Derek Scott and he had been shot down in the Western Desert. Brought over to Crete by the Italians, he had elected to be a prisoner of the Germans rather than of the Italians, and he had come on to Greece instead of going to Italy. He gave us up-to-date news of the fighting in the Middle East. It was very cheering to hear of the enormous increase in aircraft which was already paving the way for victory.

Derek was a lively figure in a crowd which had become a trifle lethargic under the strain of captivity. He and I started to plan escape. Life took on fresh lustre as we plotted the ways and means to freedom. For some time we could see no immediate prospects. Then, one day, Derek discovered that two of the medical orderlies, staff-sergeants Bill Gamble and Ted Bryant, had gained possession of the key to a door in the administration block which led to the outside street.

It was now a matter of arranging to get into the administration block by some means or another, and then hiding in this room till dusk, when our departure would be invisible to the sentries at the main gate. Hope sprang to life and I took fresh interest in exercise. I must get fit immediately so that I could go with them. Our plans after getting out of the camp were somewhat vague. We had no idea where to go, but the main thing, we felt, was to get out of the camp. After that something would happen perhaps, or we could persuade some Greeks to take us in and hide us till a further chance appeared.

From some of the Greek officers, who were interned with us, we discovered that the bridge across the Struma was very closely guarded. It would be impossible, they said, to get over it or to cross the river anywhere else. It was in flood after the snows, and would be impassable till late in the summer. Fresh information came from an Australian sergeant who had escaped months earlier and who had been recaptured suffering from acute malaria. He told us that the people were starving everywhere and that there was no way out of the country. He said he and some others had been trying continuously for more than six months. They had worn through their army boots and their clothes were in rags. They had to live in the hills in the open. Malaria was certain in northern Greece. There were no boats left, not even rowing-boats. Sooner or later recapture was certain if you lived long enough.

But we persisted. It would be different for us. We would manage, somehow, where the others had failed. In the meantime, we should wait until the cold weather passed. Snow and ice would not make our task easy. Besides, the later we left it, the more chance of obtaining food; the early harvest started about the end of May. And we should have time to prospect for friends outside who would shelter us.

As the days passed, however, the cold began to gain ground and our lowered resistance fought a losing battle for life. Dick Mann became very seriously ill, his leg flared up and poured poison into his system. It was clear that he would not last much longer under these circumstances. Others were in much the same state. The doctors fought for us; they complained repeatedly to the Commandant about the conditions. Eventually, the authorities agreed to transfer sixteen of us to one of their own military hospitals nearby. I was included, partly because of my low state of health, and partly to keep Dick company. I was sorry to go in some ways, as I realised that it compromised my chances of escape with the others, but it was clear to me that, in my present state of health and with two useless arms, I should only be a burden to them and possibly spoil their chances of getting away. So I went with mixed feelings of disappointment and relief.

Derek promised to keep in touch with me about his plans, in case it might be possible for me to stage an escape from my new quarters at the same time as them. But the doctors were very gloomy about my prospects. It would be suicide, they said, for me to attempt to live in the open in my condition and after what I had been through. I should catch pneumonia under the least provocation, and I was unfit to walk for longer than half an hour at a time anyway. Moreover, with two helpless arms, I would be dependent on the others and would just compromise their chances. Nevertheless, Norman Rose quietly gave me his army raincoat with an encouraging pat on the back, and the ever-cheerful Macnamara presented me with an army compass which he had secreted in his kit through all these months.

The faithful Lewis and Hudson, my men who had tended me with such loyalty and care for so long, were not allowed to come with me. I should have to find someone else to shave and wash and dress me. I said good-bye to them and to others of my men with heartfelt gratitude and real regret. We were told that we should see each other again. I was only to be a short distance away and we understood that occasional visits would be allowed. So it was "au revoir" and not "good-bye". Nevertheless, there was something in me which told me that it would be long before I saw them again. Dick and I drove off in our ambulance to the unknown.

VI

SALONIKA — ESCAPE TO LIVE

I

The hospital was about a mile away from the prison camp. It had been a hospital in pre-war days and was properly designed and equipped for the purpose. It was the first real hospital we had been in. It was a large stone building with a central court-yard and it had a twelve-foot wall round three sides. The fourth side was normally open to the street, but the Germans had put up a barbed-wire fence here, and the one entrance was guarded by sentries. The high wall had broken glass on top of it, just in case anyone should try to climb it. At first sight it looked as though my chances of escaping would be very slender.

Dick was carried on his stretcher up to the first floor. I walked with him. We were escorted along polished corridors redolent with hospital smells, antiseptic and ether, to a small room at the end. This was to be our home and prison. The windows were barred and the door was to be locked. We deposited Dick, who was suffering intense agony from his leg, and made him comfortable. Our doctors and orderlies bustled about with pillows and bandages and cotton wool. A German sister supervised the arrangements through an interpreter.

I was allowed to go downstairs again with the doctors to see the men into their quarters. There were fourteen of them and they had been allocated a ward to themselves on the ground floor. We settled them into their beds. The doctors left. They were to remain with the others in the camp. There were two medical orderlies left to look after us. They lived with the men in the ward. I stayed down there with them until the

German doctor made his appearance. As we waited, we contrasted our conditions with those from which we had just come. This place was clean. It was warm. There were sheets on the beds. The windows were unbroken and opened and shut. The electric light worked. It was almost too good to last.

An orderly opened the door and shouted an order. We were silent. The head doctor swept in accompanied by the usual hospital retinue. There was the sister and a couple of nurses and an orderly or two. An officer with his arm in a sling was with them. He spoke perfect English. He asked who was in charge. I stepped forward, and we advanced round the ward. At each bed I described the patient's injuries. I knew them all well; the men were all old friends. As we came to one bed, the doctor exclaimed "schwartz". I replied firmly "British". It was a gallant Maori lad who had a huge wound in his stomach. We reached the end of the ward. I was asked what was wrong with me and explained. The doctor nodded curtly and the procession swept out again.

Almost immediately, there was a call for our orderlies. They came back with a smiling Greek nurse and food. We looked at it in amazement and delight. It was stew with real meat in it. And potatoes! I saw that all was well and that the boys were going to be looked after properly. The friendly Greek nurse would see to that. I left them and went upstairs again to our little room. Here, another Greek nurse was serving Dick and myself with the same delicious stew. She was charming, but spoke no English, and had obviously been ordered not to try to speak to us. Left to ourselves we ate ravenously.

It was not long before we discovered the general set-up of the hospital. It was staffed by German doctors and sisters, aided by nurses from the Greek Red Cross. Cleaning and odd jobs were done by Greek labour. The hospital held about three hundred beds of which all but a very few were occupied by German sick and wounded. Most of the wounded came from the Afrika Corps. They were evacuated from North Africa by air via Crete. Some would be sent on for treatment in Germany.

Others would go back to their units after a spell in a local convalescent camp.

It was strange to be so closely surrounded by one's enemies. We were objects of much curiosity to the German patients. They were not allowed to speak to us but they took every opportunity to pass by our door when it was open to see these wild men from the other side. It was strange too to be looked after by German doctors and nurses. They were very correct and treated us extremely efficiently. But there was no fraternisation. To do them justice it is fair to say that they did not fraternise with their own patients either. The sisters were highly efficient professionals and stood no nonsense from anyone.

The hospital routine was similar to hospital routine anywhere. We were roused at an early hour in the morning by one of the Greek nurses. She would wash us, in cold water. Then there would be breakfast. This consisted of four half slices of bread with a kind of sour jam spread on them. And the usual ersatz coffee made from roast acorns without either milk or sugar. But this was luxury to us; it was as much food as we had had in a whole day before.

Then there would be the doctor's rounds. These were preceded by a tour of inspection by the German sister. Everything had to be spotlessly clean and tidy. The floor had been scrubbed by a Greek charwoman, the beds had been made by a Greek nurse. The final touches were made by the sister. The doctor's rounds were very formal. The door would be opened by an orderly. Then the procession would come in. Dressings would be taken off. The wounds inspected. Sometimes the doctor would attend to Dick personally. The gaping wounds in his thigh were packed with yards of gauze. Each day this had to come out and be replaced by fresh gauze after the wound had been washed and syringed with antiseptic. It was quite a long process, and invariably agonising for Dick. Usually it would be done by the German sister helped by a German orderly and the Greek nurse.

I had very little to be done to me at this stage. Every other day the dressings would be taken out of my wounds and replaced by fresh ones. The shoulder wound was closing at last and my right arm was in plaster where the wound could not be touched. It was allowed to fester away under the plaster until this became so soaked with pus that it had to be changed. This treatment was common to both sides. It had been discovered during the Spanish War that many wounds healed best by being totally encased in plaster and left immobilised for six weeks or so at a time. So I escaped lightly from these daily ordeals.

Lunch was served at about midday. It was always a thrill to see what we should get. The diet was plain but varied and good. Some days it would be a good stew with meat and potatoes and vegetables in it. Other days it would be fresh fish and potatoes. Sometimes we would get a glass of Greek red wine with it. Other times we would be permitted to buy a bottle of German beer from the canteen through a German orderly.

I fed myself these days. My left hand could reach my mouth with an effort. Dick was also able to feed himself. He was very weak and ill and obsessed and tortured by his leg. He was almost unaware of his surroundings. And he had a very poor appetite. I used to finish off what he could not take.

In the afternoon, to begin with, I was confined to our room and used to spend the time sleeping or just lying on my bed gazing at the ceiling. Dick would lie silent too, or sleeping fitfully with little groans and cries. It was rarely that we chatted these days since he was too ill to waste energy on anything but the fight for existence. We understood each other perfectly and we knew all there was to know about each other anyway; and there was little news or fresh events to discuss.

As the weeks went by, however, I gradually extended my permissible activities. I was allowed to go downstairs to visit the men; first with an escort, but later the escort was dispensed with. Then I was allowed to go out into the courtyard in the sun. First with an escort; then the escort got tired of following me around every day, and I went unaccompanied. Finally, I succeeded in getting as far as the hospital grounds and was allowed to walk round, inside the wall of course, first escorted and then, because the escort got bored, by myself. So each afternoon I would stroll gently round the hospital in the sunshine among the German wounded. The sentries on the gate kept an eye on me. Anyway, I was crippled and could not climb the wall in full view of everybody. So the authorities became accustomed to seeing me taking my exercise of an afternoon quite unaccompanied.

The next meal was served about six o'clock. It consisted of four half-slices of bread spread with either butter or white lard. With it was a slice of German sausage about half an inch thick and three inches in diameter. It was extremely tasty. And, of course, the usual coffee. After it, we would just lie in bed waiting for darkness and "lights out". Sometimes I would spend the evening, or part of it, with the men, chatting to this or that one. But frequently Dick and I just lay, idly dreaming, he in agony of body, I in frustration of mind. The shadows would deepen as evening drew on; the darkness matched our mood.

II

The room was dark. The starlight showed up the iron bars outside the window. Beyond was the wall and the great world outside. A patrol marched round from time to time and sentries watched the wire in front. So near to freedom and yet so far. Across the room, I could hear Dick's heavy uneven breathing. His tortured body lay in deep drugged sleep. He stank with the sickly sweet odour of pus. In the ward below, men fought for sleep as one of them groaned and whimpered and blasphemed his weary way out of life. Back in the prison-camp the others would be asleep. It was ten o'clock on the evening of the 10th of February 1942.

Somehow I could not sleep. Usually I had little difficulty but this was one of these nights when the mind takes control and roves restlessly round. It carried me back through these long months in prison to days of battle and, beyond, to the wasted years before the war. It dwelt a moment there, long enough to see how selfish my life had been and to savour the despair of hopelessness about myself. It went back further and searched through childhood for the gleams of light which had illumined some of those days. Memories of laughter and of love, of the family and of home, were these intangibles to be lost for ever? Or was there something, just round the corner? I longed for home, the place where you loved and where your love was returned. I longed to be free — from prison, yes, but also from myself!

With that, my mind carried me to one day when my brother had arrived home on holiday. The difference in him was striking. We had always been close to each other and done things together. But recently we had not seen much of each other as his job and mine had taken us to opposite ends of the country. I came home for some leave and he had managed to get back for a week-end. The first thing I had noticed about him was that he was radiantly happy. He had a new kind of self-confidence and everything he did was purposeful and seemed part of a programme. We used to lie late in bed and come to breakfast in our dressing-gowns. Now he was up with the lark and had made his own bed before breakfast. This small thing was typical of the great change in him. He was obviously thinking differently, but he was also acting differently.

I soon found out what it was. He told me he had met the Oxford Group and that he had decided to let God run his life from then on. He did not have to tell me that this decision had already made a remarkable difference to him. Moreover, I had seen a similar change take place in my cousin, George Marjoribanks. Unlike David, he had always been very good. He had changed from what I thought was a prig into a delightful human. He was no less good, but much more attractive. He used to say of himself before, "My friends could never make me drunk, but I could never make them sober." Now he was effective. And he had the same unusual glow and warmth and freedom that I noticed in David. It was obvious to me that there was something superhuman about this. It was not just a change of conduct, but a radical change of character that had taken place.

Both my father and mother spoke in glowing terms of the work which the Oxford Group was doing. It was a world-wide force of men and women effectively at work in many countries changing both people and policies. Its programme of Moral Re-Armament was launched in 1938. Its founder, a distinguished American, Dr. Frank N. D. Buchman, believed that the future of civilisation itself was at stake. "If you want an answer for the world today," he said, "the best place to start is with yourself. When man listens, God speaks; when man obeys, God acts; when men change, nations change. Until we deal with human nature thoroughly and drastically on a national scale, nations must still follow their historic road to violence and destruction."

Like millions of others, however, I was blind to the march of history. At that time, in 1936, I thought that he was unduly pessimistic. I did not see the underlying clash of faiths which was everywhere undermining the moral strength of nations. I failed to appraise the significance of Nazism and Communism, which were steadily gaining ground and power across the world, and which would shortly plunge us into world war and an era of ideological conflict whose outcome is still in doubt today.

What I did realise at that time was that these remarkable people presented me with a powerful moral challenge. Was I prepared to change where change was clearly due in my own life? Both David and George referred to absolute moral stand-ards — honesty, purity, unselfishness and love. "Measure your life by these," they said, "and you will see where you need to change. Then, decide to let God have complete control of you, and He will make you different."

I did not have to think long to know that if I made this bold decision there were a number of things I should have to stop doing. There were also things I was not prepared to start doing. I was a young Air Force officer. I loved the fast-moving life of the service. I was afraid to take a moral stand on obvious issues. What would my friends say? So, for these trivial personal reasons, I side-stepped the most important issue in life. I was not prepared to try and see if this way worked. It was safer and more comfortable to go on as I was doing and to believe that there was no such person as God, and no need to be any better than I was.

Now, in Salonika, six years later, the challenge caught up with me again. Face to face with apparently insoluble problems in myself and my friends, my previous objections seemed no longer relevant. There was nothing that I was not prepared to do to be free. What if there was a God? Who could make me different? Who could set me free? Who could bring me home? Or bring home to me?

I decided to try. As I lay there in the darkness and despair of my prison cell, far from home, I gave myself and all I had to God — for better or for worse, for richer or for poorer, in sickness and in health, for ever. I entrusted Him with my life, my possessions, my career, and my family and friends. I committed myself to choose what was right to do and to be, from then on, in so far as I could honestly see it.

At that moment of decision, God spoke to me. It was as though, by that simple act of the will, I had switched on the light in a dark room. I saw the meaning of things for the first time. With an intense thrill, my mind told me "God is Love." I began to see what that meant for me. My heart filled and overflowed. This was home at last, where you loved and were loved beyond all knowing. Nothing could ever separate me from it, so long as I chose to stay there. I was free at last, and no walls, or sentries, could take my freedom from me, so long as I chose to be free.

I found myself praying, a thing I had not done for ten years or more. Words came quite naturally to me and as I spoke the answer came to me. The Lord's Prayer came to my lips. It came not as a form of words but as an expression of thought and feeling. I was ecstatically happy and tears of joy flowed down my face. The experience continued for some time. Later, I lay in utter peace and quiet. I was sure and secure in the belief that now I knew the secret of living.

Before I went off to sleep I had the idea that I should test God just to make quite sure. I thought of my right hand whose fingers were doubled up and useless. I seized the little finger and prayed that it might be made straight, as a sign. Then I wrenched at it till it was numb with pain. I could not feel whether it was straight or not. So I jumped out of bed and switched on the light. It was still bent, though a trifle straighter than before. I was disappointed but not downcast. I remembered an old tale of others who had asked for a sign. I slept soundly.

When I woke, the sun was shining. The long shafts of light pierced through the branches of the trees outside the window. I opened the door and there, through the passage window, gleaming in the distance, was Mount Olympus. The massive snow-capped peak towered above the morning mists. The "home of the gods" floated in the air like a gigantic cumulus cloud. It was an exquisite morning.

People were passing in the street outside. I could see them over the wall. I watched them with new interest and feeling. Each was interesting, an individual whom I wanted to know as a friend. It was painful to see how thin some of them were. It was a joy to see some children run past, laughing. I laughed with them.

Dick was awake by now. We had always been friends, but now I felt something new and special in our relationship. I had been sorry for him in his pain, now I was sorry with him. It was a subtle difference but none the less real and new. I wanted to help him, to do things for him. We smiled at each other quietly. He was very weak and never far from overwhelming pain.

It was extraordinary how everybody seemed to be particularly delightful this day. Our two Australian medical orderlies came in to do our daily dressings, an irritating and painful process. I had come to dislike the two men heartily. Today, as they entered, I was astonished to notice immediately how nice they

94

seemed to be. We exchanged cordial greetings and joked together happily, although the dressings were no less painful. The German doctor, too, came round as usual with accompanying staff. We were accustomed to formal exchanges only. This morning he smiled and seemed friendly and I thought, "Even the Germans are nice today too"! It was some time before it finally dawned on me that it was I who had become different. An old promise had been fulfilled in me: "The Spirit of the Lord will come upon thee and thou shalt be turned into another man." "I will take away your heart of stone and give you a heart of flesh." This is the basic Christian experience which had been given me, to find love where love was not.

The result was that I found myself fascinated by people in an entirely new way. The men in the ward were a joy to talk to. They were so patient and humorous about their difficulties. Each had a home, friends, families. They loved talking of them. I had used to listen with half an ear, not really interested; now I wanted to know. My day was full of interest in this way. I could not see too much of people. I could not hear too much about them. I was interested. I cared. I was astounded with myself. I was different, and it had all happened overnight in the twinkling of an eye.

III

The full significance of what had happened to me did not strike me until some time later. Then I realised that two major problems had been solved overnight. The prisoner-of-war has two main enemies to contend with, boredom and self-pity; all prisoners fight battles on these issues. Sometimes preoccupation with escape or some hobby or education scheme keeps them from being completely overwhelmed. But this is defensive warfare and the enemy is always liable to infiltrate through even the best defences.

I had been given a clear-cut victory. As time went by I realised that I was no longer in danger from these enemies.

They had been defeated, and I was already fighting on new battlegrounds. I had no time or room to be bored or sorry for myself. I was interested in people and fully occupied in a new programme, a new daily routine which demanded my full attention and energies.

I was fascinated with my new experience and added to it daily. I found that I could speak to God and be answered instantly. I became extremely interested in the New Testament and started to read it. I found on every page something which seemed to be directly intended for me to read. The passages were so striking that I marked them with pencil. I had the idea that I would collect all these "vital" passages together in a small book which would present the secret of living to everyone in a short and easy form.

I read eagerly and it was not long before I had read through my pocket New Testament from cover to cover. It was full of pencil marks. I then had the idea that I might have missed one or two important passages from my collection, so I started to read the book again. This time I marked with blue pencil as my black lead one had disappeared. Blue and black pencil marks appeared with increasing frequency. I was astonished that I had missed so much on my first reading. Then I realised that I should have to mark everything I read. I decided that the New Testament could not be usefully abbreviated or abstracted. It was all too appropriate. So I read on and stopped marking it with pencil.

I was so interested by what I learned from day to day that I read through the whole New Testament four times in six weeks. It was entirely new to me. I had read bits of it before at home and at school. I had heard much of it read in churches from time to time. But now there was something different about it. Then it had been a fine story told in lovely old English. Now it was my own experience interpreted and foretold for me with daily directions as to what to do next. "Ye cannot serve God and Mammon." "Seek ye first the Kingdom of God and his righteousness; and all these things shall be added unto you."

"Ask, and it shall be given you; seek, and ye shall find; knock, and it shall be opened unto you." "Not every one that saith unto me, Lord, Lord, shall enter into the Kingdom of heaven; but he that doeth the will of my Father which is in heaven."

These instructions related to things I was doing or, frequently, not doing in the hospital. I was quickly aware that I had not been given my experience for nothing. Others were in just as great need of it as I. So, against my natural inclination, I began to tell people about what I had discovered. I told the men in the ward that they would have the same experience if they followed the same recipe. Some may have done so; I never knew. I had not yet realised that you need more than personal experience to be useful to other people. You need to express it in terms which they understand and apply to their own conditions.

Then there were practical things. I was slack about taking exercise. I walked when I felt like it and stopped when I wanted to. I realised that this was indulgent and inefficient. Thereafter I walked to a programme, increasing my time slowly till I was able to keep going for two hours on end without resting. I found fresh joy in fighting for fitness, and daily there was the deep satisfaction of victory and accomplishment.

The Germans could not understand me. I strode up and down the side of the hospital every day, and was so obviously enjoying it. The other patients, both German and our own men, strolled about idly, and were bored. I walked with a purpose and enjoyed it. I was getting into training for the next stage on the road to freedom.

As I walked, I thought about escape. Was it the right thing to do or should I stay with my companions? There was much to be said on both sides. Escape was adventure. It had prospects, however small, of reaching home. It was my duty to try. Or was it? Was it just selfish and liable to bring reprisals on the others? Remaining in prison would be no hardship now that I knew how to be happy; I might be able to help many to the same experience. It would be safer to count on repatriation for getting home. Was it fair to my family to risk my life escaping?

Was I not proposing suicide to try to escape in my condition? Would it be against the Geneva Convention to escape from a hospital? These and many other arguments for and against escape crossed my mind. There was only one solution, to try to find out what God wanted; I was sure He would tell me. Instantly I knew it was right for me to try to escape, whatever it might be for others. I had no guarantee of success; I had every human reason to expect failure; but I knew that for me it was the right thing to do. It was my duty to my King and also to my God. I was no longer in doubt except on the questions of when and where and how. These remained for some future decision. I had no feeling that I should go immediately. My task for the present was to get fit and to keep my eyes open for the chance which I knew would come.

As I walked round the hospital, I made a careful survey of possible routes of escape. The wire would not be difficult to get over were it not for the sentries who watched it by day and night. The wall was much too high for me to attempt to climb with two disabled arms. There was one place, however, by a door at the back of the hospital, now barred, where some iron palings led into the wall and afforded a slight prospect of success. It would require phenomenal feats of balance to get up and over twelve feet of wall, but it might just be possible. I looked at it with the practised eye of a mountaineer. If my arms had been all right it would have been easy.

One other place looked promising. It was over by a small building away from the main block, which was used as a dentistry. I was not normally allowed to go over to it even though it was inside the wall. So I decided to have my teeth seen to. I applied to see the dentist and was given the necessary permission. As I arrived at the building I paused for a moment by the door and tried to look disinterested. I was in full view of the sentry by the gate and there were other Germans even closer.

I had a quick look at the place. I saw that the main wall was joined here by another which ran in towards it at right angles.

It was only about four feet from the top of the second wall to the top of the main one. There was broken glass here as usual but it could be overcome by using suitable padding. The place looked promising. I went inside and had my interview with the dentist. It was not as bad as I had feared. He cleaned off a lot of tartar very efficiently and did a small stopping with obvious skill. He was a pleasant young man who spoke quite good English; he never thought to ask why I had come to him with so little wrong. The stopping was a temporary one and I had to come back to have it replaced later. This suited my purpose admirably. It would give me the chance for further study of the wall.

As I walked away, I noticed that you could step easily on to the top of the second wall and thence walk along it to the junction with the main wall. The only drawback was that the whole stretch was in full view of the sentry at the gate who was only about fifty yards away.

A few days later I repeated my visit and confirmed what I had first seen. I was not sure if I should be able to swing my leg over the wall at the junction. It might be just too high. If that was so, it would be just too bad. Moreover, I had no idea how big a drop there was on the other side. The ground on the outside of the wall varied in distance from the top and was frequently different to the inside level. However, from studying the houses that lay close to the wall at that point, it seemed that the drop would be about nine feet. I felt I could stand that all right in spite of my condition.

IV

About the beginning of March, Dick had a serious relapse. He became very weak and hardly conscious. His temperature was high and his leg became hard, as poison accumulated in fresh pockets. It was already open in several places with rubber tubes running in to the bone to drain off the pus; these did not seem to be adequate. The doctor decided to operate again.

One of our own doctors was invited to attend the operation to see that it was properly done, in case Dick died under the anaesthetic. Blood transfusions were also required. Typically, David Leak gave his blood together with one of the orderlies. Then he stood by to see the operation. It was successful. They put in fresh drains and poison poured out. Dick's temperature fell. But more transfusions were needed to keep him going. A German corporal from the next ward, who had a wound in the arm, volunteered. But David Leake was there again as donor and the other doctors joined in with many of the orderlies to supply the vital plasma. Day by day Dick was wheeled out to the theatre to have these transfusions. Every move was torture to him.

There was little that I could do for him practically. My helpless arms were a handicap. But I longed to be able to help him. I felt strongly that I could help by praying for him. I did this constantly. I also felt I could help by being cheerful and sensitive to his mood, when he was suffering to be silent, and when he was able to chat, to take his mind as far as possible from our environment. We talked of his home and of mine, of happy days and amusing episodes of the past. Dick had a wonderful sense of humour which came to the top under the most trying circumstances.

The 3rd of March was his birthday. In the morning, he was carried out as usual to the operating theatre. I lay thinking of him and asked God to give him his life and health again. I had an extraordinary feeling of certainty that all would be well with him. I called for our Greek nurse. Anni was a delightful girl who looked after us with special attention. I suggested to her that a bottle of champagne would be suitable for the occasion. She went off enthusiastically and came back soon after with a bottle. I had no idea where it had come from and did not ask. I paid for it gratefully and secreted it in my bed. Dick was wheeled in later.

That evening we celebrated. There were Anni, and Tom and Bill, the two orderlies, and myself. Dick was delighted as we drank his health. And in some mysterious way there was a special supper for him. It was a memorable occasion. From then on he began slowly to recover.

The Greek nurses were a very fine lot of girls. They were volunteers who had joined the Greek Red Cross and nursed the wounded from the Albanian Front earlier in the war. Then the Germans had come. Some of them had been in hospitals taken over by the Germans. True to the traditions of the Red Cross, these girls had stayed on to nurse whatever wounded came in. They were paid by the Greek Red Cross a sum which, as the currency rapidly inflated, became quite ridiculously small. And the German authorities refused to allow them any food, even though they were looking after German wounded.

They would have starved had it not been for their patients. Fortunately, the German wounded were not so heartless as their authorities. While the sister turned a discreet back on the proceedings, a patient would go round each ward with a plate collecting food for the Greek nurses. This would then be smuggled out to them and eaten in the lavatories.

For a long time Anni was our day nurse. She was nice looking and gay and cheerful. She worked extremely hard and was a tower of strength to us in all sorts of ways. She was not allowed to talk to us and had been chosen to look after us because she spoke no English. But we picked up a little Greek and I spoke a little German and we were able to make ourselves understood. Unfortunately the authorities discovered that she was friendly to us and she was dismissed from the hospital in disgrace.

Then there were two Russians who used to look after us as night nurses. They both spoke English and French and we were able to talk more freely to them. One was an elderly lady who had escaped from Russia during the Revolution and had been living in Salonika ever since. She was a skilled nurse and was very good to us, taking special care of Dick. The younger one was also a very good friend to us. At one time I contemplated being sheltered by some family in Salonika after escaping, until I should be fit or possibly get away on some boat. I went as far as to ask this girl to look out for a place for me. She willingly took on the job. In the end, I decided that it would not be right to use or compromise the nurses in any way, as the Germans would be sure to suspect them of complicity. So we abandoned that scheme.

I had also been keeping a close watch on the lorries and carts and even hearses which came in to the hospital from time to time for various reasons. The refuse cart was one which I contemplated hiding in. It would not have been easy as a watch was kept on all these vehicles from the time they entered to the time they left again. It would have to be an odd chance to board one while no one was looking.

Early in March, during a visit from the doctors to give a blood transfusion to Dick, Derek Scott managed to be included on the party from the camp. He had to give his parole in order to come so he could not use the occasion to escape. But he told me that he and the two medical orderlies were all ready to go and intended to make a break on the 7th. He invited me to join them if I was able to get out then.

The scheme looked very attractive. I should have three stalwart friends to help me in the long trek to freedom. So we arranged a meeting place high on the hill above Salonika. We were to escape as near to eight o'clock in the evening as possible. Whoever got away first would wait for the others at the appointed rendezvous till midnight. Then he would be free to go on by himself if necessary.

On the 6th I developed a severe blister on my heel from walking and was unable to put on my boots. In addition I was unwell and had a temperature. I prayed about it and felt convinced that I had been wrong to consider handicapping the others with my presence. I sent word back to the camp through one of our visitors that I should not be able to join them.

They made a successful getaway on the 7th through the door, more or less as planned. They had to get out quickly, and in daylight, as they were in danger of being discovered where they were hiding in the administration block. But somehow

102

the sentries did not see them and they walked away to the hills without incident.

There was a terrific fuss made and the Germans searched everywhere for them. The regulations were tightened up and the Commandant was sacked. Poor old Severin. He came round to the hospital to say good-bye to us, especially to his farmer friend Dick. He was off to the Russian Front as a punishment. We were sorry to see him go as he had been a reasonable man and conditions had been bearable while he was there. Now, under his successor, things became very bad indeed. The food shortage was acute even by old standards. We had exhausted the supplies of Red Cross parcels for the time and it was some weeks before more arrived. The men were driven to catching cats to put in the stew and there were fights over bread issues.

At the hospital we escaped these privations. We used to save food for our visitors from the camp. They were ravenously hungry when they came to see us. The Greek nurses helped to obtain food for them from the kitchens when they came to give blood donations. Taking blood from starving men was a cruel necessity. We would gladly have given ours but the long months of illness had left us even weaker than them. I was still some fifty to sixty pounds under my normal weight, and my blood pressure was very low.

V

The sun was shining. Away in the distance it glistened on the high snows on Mount Olympus. It was warm in the countryard of the hospital as I strolled round chatting to some of our men. There was David Blair from Dundee, a private in the famous Black Watch regiment who had a serious leg wound which refused to heal. Then there was Albert Moore of my squadron whose terrible injuries were starting to heal now that he was able to get better food. They were sitting in the sun as usual.

It was a typical scene. The courtyard was full of men sunning themselves. Some were in bed with the bedclothes back so that their wounds were exposed to the life-giving sunlight. There was a priest among the German wounded who had a bad arm from a wound received in the Western Desert. He had been a stretcher-bearer. He was a nice fellow and had lent me his Bible for a day. I was interested to see it as it had a map showing the journeys of Saint Paul. I had studied the Apostle's wanderings with a sympathetic and careful eye. The contours of the coast line had a fascination which was not entirely historic.

He came up to me and suggested playing a game of chess. I declined as gracefully as I could. I had other plans. That morning the authorities had informed me that we were to be sent by hospital train to Germany early the next morning, the 28th March. They warned me to be ready to go.

This precipitated a crisis for me. I had already felt that God wanted me to try to escape. It had only been the timing and details which had been left unclear. Now, I walked to and fro on my usual exercise programme and prayed for further guidance. I also prayed to be kept willing for whatever course might seem indicated, whatever the consequences might be for me personally. After a struggle to lay down my preferences, both for relative comfort and security on the one hand and for freedom and adventure on the other, my conviction grew that this was the day. My inner voice said, "Tonight, half an hour after dusk". My mind was clear, it was now or never.

During the morning I surreptitiously brought my few belongings down to the men's ward and distributed them among the men. I had already given Dick some of them. I was well equipped with clothes as my first Red Cross clothes parcel had arrived from home appropriately enough on the 21st of March, the day before my birthday. So I had a small surplus of shirts and woollen things which I could not carry with me.

I also brought down my army raincoat, the gift of Norman Rose, and stored it under Albert Moore's bed. The pockets were crammed full of things. I had a razor and soap, toothbrush and toothpaste. Then there were woollen gloves and a helmet. There were a mosquito net and two spare pairs of socks. I had also about two pounds of chocolate saved up, and the medical orderlies prepared a box of drugs for me with fifty tablets of aspirin, quinine and sulphanilamide.

I talked over my prospects with my friends. They did not look healthy. I was still very weak and unfit. My left shoulder had closed up by now, but only recently, and the arm was stiff and weak and only capable of being used for feeding and dressing myself. My right forearm was still open and discharging after ten months' treatment. It was out of plaster but was quite useless and wrapped in bandages. After ten months of prison hospitals and serious illness I was unlikely to have much reserve of strength or resistance to hard conditions. The medical orderlies thought I was crazy to attempt to escape in that condition and said so.

Certainly the prospects outside were unpromising. Greece was starving and people were falling down and dying of starvation in the streets of Salonika. We were told that all routes out of the country were very carefully guarded by now. It had been easier earlier on perhaps, but by now the Germans had strict control of the small boat traffic and also the passes and bridges. The frontier with Turkey was closely guarded and there was reputed to be a neutral zone of some miles in width where both sides shot at strangers. There was still snow on the hills and the rivers were in flood.

Also I had no friends outside with whom I could get in touch. I spoke practically no Greek. I had no map or definite plans. I had no one with me to help and would not be able to fend for myself with my useless arms. I could not possibly disguise myself as a Greek or as anything except myself. All these arguments and more were advanced to dissuade me. But I knew what I must do. I was extremely doubtful of my chances of survival, far less of escape, but the choice was more than one of expediency. The whole of my new way of life hung in the balance. Either I followed what I believed was right to do or I went back to a life dictated by self-interest and self-will. It was a choice of life or death. It seemed that I must choose death to live.

In fact I would much rather have died than face going back to the dreary, desperate existence I had endured before my fateful decision in February. So, while I considered seriously all the arguments put forward by my friends against escaping, I remained convinced it was the right course.

I was surprised, to say the least of it, therefore, when at midday my temperature suddenly rose from normal to a high fever. I thought it must be a sign from heaven that I was choosing the wrong thing. So I retired, puzzled and despondent, to bed. I had been sincere in my belief that it was right for me to go. Why had I been wrong? As I pondered and prayed, I realised that my fever did not make the slightest difference to the rightness or wrongness of the case. It only made what had been an extremely difficult task a little more impossible. Humanly, it would be utter folly to start an adventure of this type with a fever. It was probably the usual osteomyelitis temperature indicating a flare up in one of my wounds. I was accustomed to that. But it could not be regarded as a good start for an escape. It was a clear choice of expediency or principle. This time I chose principle. I should try to do what seemed right, no matter what it cost. I had to trust God to take care of me. It seemed that He wanted me to adventure in faith as well as in fact — to make an act of faith as well as one of obedience.

I felt sick and had a splitting headache but, now that my way was clear, I was strangely at peace. Come what may I would escape to live. The afternoon passed and our evening meal arrived. I did not feel hungry but I ate it just the same. I might need all the food I could carry. The shadows lengthened as dusk drew on. I had an empty feeling in the pit of my stomach as before my first solo flight.

Dick did not argue with me. He knew me and was fully aware of what I had been thinking and doing these latter days. He chattered of this and that. We smiled at each other. If only he could have come too. I got ready to go and laced up my boots with care. They were Australian army boots in perfect condition and had belonged to Dick. He would not need them now.

Dick said that he had not prayed for years, but he would pray for me now. I was deeply touched and thanked him, suggesting that he should also pray for himself. I could wish him nothing better than the experience which I had found. He promised to. We wisecracked each other and I promised to visit him in Australia. With that I opened the door and moved into adventure.

It was quarter-past eight in the evening. Normally at that hour the corridors would have been crowded with Germans. I was astonished to find no one in sight. I walked down the corridor towards the main stairs. I met nobody. At the stairs I paused, hesitating. There was still no one in sight. I went on down, my boots making what seemed a tremendous noise on the bare wood. At the foot I stopped and listened. The hum of the hospital was all that I could hear. There seemed to be no one in the lower corridors either. I felt that this was a miracle, but I knew that I could not succeed without miracles so I went on hopefully. I covered the thirty yards or so of corridors to the men's ward without meeting a soul. Perhaps they were all listening to an important radio broadcast. Whatever the cause the timing was perfect. God seemed to have known best and "half an hour after dusk" was proving to be miraculous guidance.

Inside the ward I found the men in their beds, excited at my venture and with all the prospects of the move in the morning. I went round the beds and said good-bye to each. I felt a little self-conscious as I realised it was quite likely that I should be brought back in again by the ear or feet first within a few minutes. However, I planned for success and went on with my farewells.

I put on my coat and was just preparing to go out when the door opened and the night nurse came in. There was a little group round me and I sat down on one of the beds. She walked straight to one of the lads in bed and gave him a sleeping draught. He drank quickly and she took the glass and walked out without even glancing in my direction. I started to breathe again and moved quickly to the door.

David Blair hobbled with me and presented me with a cloth cap he had made from odd bits of cloth. It would be very useful and I accepted it with gratitude. Albert Moore also insisted on coming to the outside door with me. The three of us crept out of the ward and across the courtyard in the bright moonlight. On the far side we entered the other wing of the hospital and went downstairs to a side door near the nurses' quarters. I had had a hunch to come this way. My hand was not strong enough to turn the handle, but David Blair tried it. By another miracle it was not locked. We opened it quietly and looked out. There was my inner wall about ten yards away, with the main wall some twenty yards further on. The moon was shining and the sentry stood at the gate about thirty yards away. He was looking straight ahead, with his rifle slung on his shoulder.

My inner voice told me to have no fear and to walk across quite naturally. I whispered goodbye to my two companions who closed the door silently behind me. Then, encouraged by the extraordinary way things seemed to have worked out already, I set off across the ash-covered roadway, my boots crunching like thunder at each step. But the sentry made no move. I walked on up a bank of grass and on to the top of the inner wall. Silhouetted against the moon, I stepped cautiously along it, my boots clattering on the stone. I felt as conspicuous as a tap dancer in the footlights and expected to be shot at any moment. But the sentry continued to gaze passively ahead although I was only about twenty degrees off his line of sight. Perhaps he was day-dreaming, away in a happier world of make-believe. The important thing for me was that, wherever his mind might be, it had at least temporarily left Salonika!

It seemed an age, but I reached the main wall at last. On my left was the dentist's building. I heard voices coming from an open window. Inside, some German soldiers were playing cards.

They were so close that I could have spat on them. Fortunately, no one looked up to where I stood, silhouetted in the moonlight above them.

The main wall now barred my path. It came up to my waist and was covered with broken glass. I swung my leg up to try to stride it, and my boot crashed loudly on the stonework. I was unable to get it over. I stood with bated breath for a moment — surely the sentry behind me must have heard that noise. But neither he nor the soldiers below appeared to have noticed it.

I tried again, quietly this time, but it was clear that the wall was too high for my leg to cross. I stood there, utterly confounded, expecting discovery at any moment.

In despair, I prayed to be shown what to do next. Should I go back? Or try elsewhere? What had I done wrong? I would do anything God told me. Even to shouting hello to the sentry if that seemed right! As soon as I had given up once more my natural demands for security and success, my fear left me. I was no longer worried about the sentry or the other soldiers. At the same time, I was strangely reassured — I had done as I had been directed up till then. I was at the right place at the right time. There must be a way.

Suddenly I realised that I could get over the wall without depending on my arms if I lay face downwards over it and wriggled my body round until I lay along it. Then I could drop off on the outside, feet first.

I quickly pulled out the woollen things in my pockets, my socks and helmet, and also my mosquito net, and put them over the broken glass. Then I leant over them. The other side of the wall was dark in the shadow of some trees and houses. I could not see the ground or how far I should have to fall. I hoped it was not more than I had judged it previously — about nine feet. I started to wriggle my body round to lie along the wall rather than across it. My arms were useless and I kicked my legs in the air in the effort to get round. This made me lose my precarious balance and I fell head first over the wall into the darkness.

I found myself standing on the ground. I had fallen on my feet and was not even conscious of any jar to my arms as I landed. As I stood there, the padding which I had put over the broken glass fell into my hands. I did not even have to stoop to pick it up.

The miracle of it all astounded me. I listened carefully for sounds of pursuit, but all was quiet. I was filled with an overwhelming sense of gratitude. I had ventured and not been let down. I knew that the adventure was just beginning and that there would be many difficulties and dangers before my long journey was over. I could not see what lay ahead nor guess that one day I should stand here again in different circumstances. All I knew then was that miracles seemed to be given to those who dare to be free. The road ahead was dark but I knew that, wherever it led, it led to new life and a new world. I had escaped from prison. Far more important, I had escaped to live.

VII

MACEDONIA – THE STAR BY NIGHT

I

It was dark down there in the alley where I had fallen to freedom. The high wall of the hospital was on one side and tall houses a few yards away shut off the moonlight. I stood still, listening. There was no sound of pursuit or commotion from the other side of the wall. My escape had been unnoticed so far. I realised slowly that I was free. Free to choose where I should go next. Free to walk where I chose. Free to live.

I drew in the cool night air in deep draughts, savouring the smells and gazing in awe at the immensity of the sky above, where the stars shimmered coldly and the soft moonlight glanced off the tops of the trees. Where to go now was the question. I referred it to God and, even as I asked, I saw the star.

It hung low in the sky and outshone every other star. Large and luminous, it was like a lamp on the distant horizon. Somehow I knew it. I remembered an old tale of wise men who had followed a star in the East. It had brought them to their journey's end in a country which I too hoped to reach. I checked up on my bearings, finding the Plough and thence the Pole Star. My guiding star lay approximately in the East.

I moved off quietly down the alley. After about fifty yards it joined the main street which ran past the hospital. I could turn left to avoid the sentries and get quickly away into the hills, or right to pass close to the wing where the men's ward was. My inclination was to get away, but I thought of them all, behind the wall and the wire, listening anxiously for the shots which would tell them that my attempt had failed. I wondered how to let them know that I was all right. I turned right and walked down the street; as I came level with the ward, I whistled as loudly as I was able. The tune was "Loch Lomond; the words which ran through my mind, somewhat inaccurately, were "I'll tak' the high road and ye'll tak' the low road, and I'll be in Scotland before ye." I knew that David Blair of the Black Watch, at least, would understand. After the war I heard that my whistling had in fact been recognised and that they had been greatly relieved to realise that I was safely out.

There were people in the main street, passing up and down in the moonlight. Some were German soldiers, others Greek civilians. My whistling was attracting attention. I strolled on, casually, past the corner by the gate where the sentry still stood motionless. A street sloped away up the hill. Above it was my star. I walked slowly on, unnoticed in the darkness, revelling in my new-found freedom, entranced with the excitement of adventure.

I walked steadily up the street till it ended on the hillside above the city among scattered houses. From there I walked on in the same direction, keeping my course fixed on the star. It led me upwards, a steep climb in places; I sat down whenever I felt tired or out of breath, and rested. These rests refreshed me and I was able to go on without undue exhaustion. I was surprised at this unexpected stamina and also to find that my temperature had obviously fallen to normal. My head was clear and I felt fine. Another miracle?

High on the hill, I sat and gazed over the twinkling lights below. The "black-out" was not very effective; there were many chinks of light to be seen and the shape of the city could be picked out quite clearly. I located the prison-camp with ease. There were the searchlights swinging alternately from one lane of wire to another. I thought of all my friends there, hungry and hopeless, as they waited for the morning and the train that was to take them to Germany.

As I sat and gazed I heard, in the distance, the baying of hounds. I thought, "They have put the dogs on my trail," and had a momentary fear. Then I realised that my "lucky" star had led me for some considerable distance along well-frequented streets. My trail must have been crossed and recrossed many times and would be quite impossible for dogs to trace. My natural inclination, to keep away from people and take to the hillside quickly, might well have been fatal. Had I known it there was, in fact, a tremendous upheaval about midnight, when my escape was discovered and reported by the night sister. For days afterwards the Germans combed Salonika in search of me.

I rose and walked on upwards with the slow rhythmic stride I had learned on mountain slopes in Scotland. Breathing to match my pace, I sucked in two breaths at each step. It was hard going, but I kept at it steadily and gained height slowly. Clouds were passing across the moon, casting great black shadows; silver-edged they slipped silently across the sky.

When the moon was hidden, it was difficult to see where to tread. Later, the clouds thickened and it became very dark. The hillside was rough with great boulders. Patches of thorn and scrub-oak grew side by side with sweet-smelling herbs, wild thyme and sage bushes. I was unconcerned and at peace. I remembered the old Scots Psalm "Thy foot He'll not let slide, nor will He slumber that thee keeps." I strode out over the rough slopes and never stumbled.

At one point I came to a little ravine. I could hear the rush of water as a mountain stream sped on its way downwards to the sea. I came to the edge of it, wondering how deep and how wide it might be. I felt I should step out blindly, trusting in the power which had so amazingly preserved me until then. My feet came down on hard stone with each step in the pitch darkness. I found myself on the other side and my feet were not even wet. I must have trodden on big stones near the surface. Foolish? Foolhardy? Yes, perhaps! I was to learn later that it was better to "leave nothing to chance and then leave everything to God." At that time, I felt that God would look after chance as well; my need was great and He did.

After some time, I came to a saddle or pass through the hills. There was a path leading through it and it was easier to walk there than over the trackless hillside. The path led in the right direction, towards my star which now could only be seen occasionally through breaks in the cloud. I walked on this path and came over the summit and out of sight of the now distant city. In the darkness, I made out the outline of a stone hut. Suddenly there was an uproar, the clamouring of many large dogs.

Sheepdogs in the Balkans have a notorious reputation. They are used as a bodyguard for the flocks, to defend them from the attacks of wolves and two-legged enemies as well. They are trained to attack anyone who approaches. The dogs are bigger than wolves and more heavily built. They have white coats, and their tails and ears are clipped close so that the wolves cannot get hold of them. They wear great leather collars studded with iron spikes to protect their throats. Each flock of goats or sheep usually has anything from half a dozen to a dozen of these dogs as escort, under orders of the shepherd, rather like a convoy of merchantmen with their escorting warships.

Pictures of the ancients often show them carrying long staffs. I used to think that these were just a type of walking-stick. No doubt they were also convenient, when they had a crook on the end, for catching sheep and goats. In fact the staff is carried primarily as a weapon against these dogs. However, I had no staff, and my hands were incapable of wielding one.

The dogs approached rapidly, their clamour filling the night air. I was frightened and did not know what to do. I prayed, not to be relieved of an awkward situation, but to be free from fear of it. I found myself immediately calm and unafraid with an inner peace and strength which I knew were not my own. I walked slowly on.

The dogs had never met this reaction before. They did not know what to do. They reached me in a noisy mob and snarled and bounded round me. But not one attacked me. Perhaps they had not made enough noise? They redoubled their efforts,

114

and the din was enough to wake the dead. I walked on, rejoicing at my release from fear. The shepherd was now within call and I shouted to him, above the din, to call off his dogs. He made no move, wondering who should be walking the hills at this time of night.

Momentarily, I doubted the whole fantastic position; I was afraid again. Simultaneously I was attacked by a scurry of dogs from behind. My trouser leg was ripped and my leg torn by fierce teeth. I shouted, this time in alarm, for help. I shouted at the dogs and bent down as if to pick up stones to throw at them. They would have come at me if the shepherd had not called them off.

I thanked him in Greek, "Efkaristo para poli." Appropriately, they were the first words I had learned. He asked me where I had come from, where I was going to. I understood, but could not reply. I said "Inglezi" and he responded warmly; he would understand the rest. I could not wait with him, nor did he invite me to, and I walked on slowly with my torn trouser leg flapping and blood trickling down my calf from the gashes made by the dogs' teeth. It was nothing to worry about if the dogs were clean and healthy. It was nippy rather than painful. But it was a lesson, and one which I should not forget.

The night was now well advanced. I had crossed the summit and was winding along among the rolling hillocks of a plateau. Soon I came to a valley. Down below I could make out the outline of a village. I was tired. It was miraculous that I had managed to keep going as long as this. Should I go in and find a bed? I was tempted to, but God told me that I should go on. So I obeyed.

The path led on round the side of the valley without losing height. Evidently it by-passed the village. I walked on slower now, and feeling very tired. I longed to lie down but was determined to go on until I dropped or until it was clear that it was the right time and place to stop. My star was out of sight now, but I knew I was still heading in the right direction. Soon the path turned down hill, off the line in which I was walking. I hesitated, long enough to pray, and then following my conviction, walked straight on across the hillside. Blind with fatigue, in the black night, on a rough mountainside, I did not know where I was going. All I knew was that miraculously I had escaped. This was a free life and I savoured it to the full. Fatigue was something to fight. The future was the great unknown, something to venture into. The high road to freedom stretched far ahead.

I stumbled, and fell flat on my back on a soft slope. My arms were unhurt and I had come to no harm. I lay resting for a while. I realised it must be very late or very early, and that my adventure was only just beginning. This was the time to sleep. The question remained, where? I did not feel that my present location was adequate. I got up and walked on expectantly. Sure enough, within a few paces, I came upon a thick bush, standing about four feet high and closely knit with fine twigs. This was the place for me. I let myself fall backwards on to it. It was very comfortable, springy and even, and I sank in far enough to be completely sheltered from the breeze. Immediately, I fell fast asleep.

II

When I woke, the sun was up, though still low in the east. The sky was clear and I looked out across rolling country to the foothills of a mountain capped with snow, its peak glistening there like a cloud. It was Mount Khortiates, and we used to see its snow cap from the prison camp. Fragile wisps of morning mist hung in the hollows. Close beside me, a lark was praising the morning in unmistakable trills of ecstasy.

I was comfortable and had slept soundly. I stretched and breathed in the brisk morning air with appreciation. The realisation that I was free came upon me again like a flood, washing away every other thought. I sat up and sang; I shouted with joy. I stood up and stretched and wondered where to go.

In front of me, a road wound north-eastwards. I walked

down the hill a short distance to it. Guided by my inner voice I turned right and walked along it in a south-westerly direction. As I walked, I sang. I felt extremely well and I was free. The road swung round the hill to the right heading back towards Salonika. It was time to leave it. I kept a careful ear and eye open for signs of motor transport which would indicate Germans on the move, perhaps search parties out looking for me on the roads. It was wise to keep to the hills.

A track led off to the left and I was once more heading east. I pulled out some chocolate and munched it as I walked along. Occasionally, I would skip or jump an obstacle for the sheer delight of living. I was a little stiff in the legs after my long climb, but the weeks of strenuous training had prepared me well. I was thin and weak, but what there was of me was fit.

The track faded out by a mountain stream. I walked upstream in the little ravine cut out of the hillside by past floods. I drank some of the water; it was fresh and clear and ice-cold. Later, I stopped by a pool and washed as thoroughly as I could, taking pains to get my feet clean and dry. I had no blisters or signs of any, thanks to the weeks of training in boots which I had felt it right to do, sometimes much against my inclination.

Leaving the stream where it was precipitous, I struck out round the side of the hill. It was hard going as the scrub-oak and thorn bushes were thick, and timber grew closely to ten and twenty feet high. It meant forcing a way through and it was bad for the clothes. My trousers were further torn in no time, but I kept on and came round the shoulder of the hill.

Facing me, on another slope, about a mile away, I saw smoke. It was a shepherd's fire. He had a big flock of goats in a thorn compound hacked out of the bush. I was over-joyed at the prospect of meeting someone. Then I thought of the dogs. But I was sure that it would be all right. I walked on with renewed energy.

When I was about a quarter of a mile from the compound, the dogs scented me and came bounding out. The shepherd looked up in surprise — he was milking his goats. I waved to him and shouted a greeting. He called off the dogs who stood back from me, snarling and yapping. I walked on and he came to meet me. I held out my hand, delighted to see him.

He led me into the compound. Thorns were piled ten feet high round an enclosure with a single gate. Inside were about a hundred goats and a small hut made of brushwood. The fire was burning by the hut. Wood smoke and goat were mixed in a strong aroma. Lying on the ground in the door of the hut I noticed an Irvin suit flying jacket, in excellent condition.

I pointed to it. He laughed and said "Inglezi". Then he picked up a filthy-looking tin can which had a capacity of about half a gallon. Rapidly seizing the nearest goat, he milked it and then another. I watched the white milk squirt through filthy hands and matted hairs and wondered what grade it would be given in England. The milk in the tin had hairs and muck floating in it. So he took another tin, as filthy as the first, put a large piece of greasy sacking across it, which had obviously been used often before for the same purpose, and filtered the milk through the sacking. I was then handed the tin with an expressive smile as much as to say, "Now! Look at all the trouble I have taken to make this perfect for you!" I could not refuse, nor did I wish to; it looked much too good.

The tin tasted horrible, but the milk was delicious. I drank and drank. We sat on either side of the fire, he squatting on his heels, I on a stone, while he broke bread. He took a loaf of hard brown bread from his pocket, broke a chunk off, and gave it to me. We smiled at each other and dipped our bread in the fresh warm milk. The sun shone on us. The shepherd was in his twenties, well built, good looking; he had Greek Army battledress trousers, and pigskin sandals on his feet. A filthy shirt and sheepskin cloak made up his wardrobe. He had a huge staff with a crook on one end. I expected him to produce shepherd's pipes and play on them, but instead he rolled a cigarette. "Apo pou isthe?" he asked. "Where are you from?"

We chatted. How? It is difficult to say. I knew only a few

words of Greek, a few more of Turkish, a little German and French. He knew a few words of English and German and French and he spoke Turkish. Between us, we talked animatedly. I learned that he had fought in Albania, that he thought less than nothing of the Italians. He had fought against the Germans too. They had been cut off and surrounded. He had been at Kalamata during the evacuation from the beaches. There he had been given the Irvin suit jacket by a British aviator. He had escaped northwards and reached home. Now he was waiting, watching his goats. Soon the English would come again. He made a fierce gesture across his throat; many Germans would have their throats cut. And Bulgarians, here there was much excitement and waving of hands. Evidently the Bulgars had a stormy time ahead of them.

He asked about me. I told him. He almost wept over my wounded arms. He asked where I was going to. I said: "Home". He smiled incredulously, I was joking. He advised me to go to Ayon Oros, the sacred Mount Athos. There I would find friendly monks who would look after me till the English came again. It was a long way and a rough road but he had heard that many English had been before me. I pricked up my ears at this and made a mental note of the name Ayon Oros. I was to hear it many times.

It seemed right for a man on a pilgrimage like mine to visit the sacred mountain, where there were many ancient monasteries. No one else could live there except the monks and those who were entering the monasteries. The peninsula was cut off from the mainland by mountains and reached by trails that only a mountaineer could follow. From the sea, the huge cliffs rose hundreds of feet from the water and the mountains towered up to the skies. On the crags and ledges were the holy men, the monks in their lonely monasteries, eking out an existence by fishing and by scraping a livelihood off the mountain slopes.

As we talked and ate our bread and milk the dogs clamoured again outside. We looked up. Away on the far slopes my shepherd friend picked out two specks. They were men approaching. They would see the smoke of our fire. I prepared to bolt in case they should be enemies in search of me, but I was restrained by my friend. He beckoned me to sit still. As the men drew nearer, I noticed with apprehension that they wore uniform and carried rifles. But my friend laughed reassuringly, so I waited with him. The men came up and shouted greetings. They were dressed in light grey uniforms and carried carbines. "Agrofilax" were the words used to describe them. I gathered that they were country police as distinct from town police. They asked my friend many questions about me and their attitude, which had been cold and suspicious at first, became slightly warmer. They asked me where I was going to, but in rather official tones, so I again replied "Home". There was general laughter.

I was not sure of these newcomers. I knew that there would be a big reward offered for my recapture. The Germans did not like losing Squadron Leaders; there would be every induce-ment to treachery. After all, these people did not know me. I was a foreigner and I was a burden on the countryside both from the point of view of possible reprisals by the Germans, and also of being an extra mouth to feed in a starving com-munity. I sensed that they were still shifty and ill at ease. I felt that it was time to leave.

The sun was high in the heavens and there was a long road ahead. I said good-bye to my shepherd friend with genuine regret and gratitude for his wonderful hospitality. He had given me of his best. To the others I was more formal but bade them a cordial farewell. I walked off northwards over the crest of the hill. As I reached the summit, I turned to wave to the now distant party. I noticed that the policemen were also pre-paring to leave, and my suspicions were somehow strengthened. I felt that there was no time to lose. I ran downhill along a goat track.

Soon I came to a road running east. As I reached it I remem-bered my star and turned along it. Walking along the road enabled me to move fast and I could see for a long way in both directions, so that I could slip off into the bush if any vehicles approached. I felt that I should put as much distance as possible between me and the police and strode out briskly.

After a time a village came in sight, nestling in the lower slopes of the mountain. It would be unwise to be seen there so I kept an eye open for a route which would by-pass it. Before long, a track led off to the north. I went along it. It meandered through scrub and stones with an occasional vineyard or small patch of cultivation. But I encountered nobody. I came to a dip, down to a mountain stream. By the gravel ford there was a patch of green turf. The sunlight danced on the swift-flowing stream. Little wild flowers gleamed like jewels in the sward. I felt suddenly tired; this was the place to rest. I bathed my feet in the stream and turned my socks out in the sun. Then I lay on the grass; cool breezes and the chatter of the burn lulled me to sleep.

III

The sun was still up when I woke, but I lay in the shade. My face was glowing pleasantly from the exposure to the sun. It was late afternoon and getting cool. I put on my boots and set off once more.

The track led eastward again now and climbed steeply up the spur of the mountain. I made a steady pace for an hour or two. The scene was beautiful. The mountain mass rose on my right in wooded slopes. On my left, I looked out across rolling country down to a lake in the distance. The lake was large, about twelve miles long and four miles wide. Small boats dotted the surface dragging the depths for fish. Food was life and fortune in a starving land.

I walked steadily through the cool evening air, relishing the signs of spring everywhere. The wild flowers were growing in profusion on every mossy bank, and the streams were in flood from the melting snow higher up the mountain. Later, I came round a spur to find a village clinging to the hillside just below.

My guidance was that this one would be all right to enter. It was just a collection of whitewashed houses lining a single, steep cobbled street. At the top was a simple little church. A stream ran down the street to join another just below the village. I debated whether to try to find a bed there. I had a hunch that I should, but an ambition to get further on that night. There would be another village within an hour's walking; I could see it in the distance.

Undecided, I walked on down the hill. As I entered the village I was quickly surrounded by a crowd of men, women and children. We greeted each other and I was barraged with questions. "Inglezi" was the word I repeated most often and it had a good effect. Everybody would smile and repeat it to one another. Then the babble would rise to a crescendo again.

I paraded slowly down the cobbled street. Stopping half-way I sat down and chatted with a group of men. There were the usual questions, where I was going and where from; every-body was friendly and everybody seemed to have fought with the English and also in Albania. There were no Germans here, only a patrol which visited the village from time to time. But if they were to harbour an escaped British prisoner there would be terrible trouble. There would be shooting and the village would be burned down.

I hesitated to ask whether it would be possible to house me for a night somewhere. Eventually, I decided to go on to the next village. In some ways it was easier than to ask a difficult question. So I got up and went on my way. I bade them fare-well and they waved to me as I sauntered on down the street to the river. At the ford I hesitated again. It was getting near dusk. I was tired. But I felt it would make me look foolish to go back now and, on this somewhat doubtful decision, I went firmly ahead.

The path rose steeply again round another spur of the moun-tain. Every few hundred yards there would be a fork and I had to choose which to take. I never knew where the tracks led, so that my choice was always a little precarious. Eventually, as evening closed in and I was more and more weary, I let myself drift to whichever fork in the trail happened to lie straight in front of me when I opened my eyes. After some time, as the dusk deepened, I realised that I was lost.

The realisation came as a shock. I had been trusting blindly in Providence and not using my own faculties to help. I realised that this was wrong, but I resisted the suggestion that I was to blame. I decided to find my way back to the village from which I had just come. But it was easier said than done. The goat tracks crossed and recrossed each other in a maze among the thick scrub and rocks. The hillside here was very steep, which added to my difficulties. I found myself at the foot of a precipitous gulley with a torrent rushing down it. Negotiating my way round crags and boulders in daylight was not easy without the use of my arms; at night it was a thousand times worse. I fell repeatedly and each time I stumbled I felt less inclined to get up again.

In the darkness, I lay in a wood. The ground was wet and the weather was blowing up towards what looked like a storm. I had tripped up over a fallen tree and was near the end of my tether. I was quite exhausted. I wondered what to do next, whether to get up and go on or lie there till daylight. I decided that the situation was out of my control, if indeed it had ever been in it. God must decide and tell me what to do. Once more I was willing to try anything. Immediately, I felt I should go on for a little, something would turn up.

I got up and staggered on. I had not gone for more than a few minutes when I saw the light of a fire, quite near, a little way up the hill. I made for it, rejoicing that, once more, I had not been let down. Dogs greeted me as usual, but I was too tired to notice them and they were called off. The fire was outside a brushwood hut and four men were seated round it. They were shepherds and their flocks were shut out into a compound nearby. I was covered in mud and dishevelled as I staggered into the firelight. I sat down and tried to answer some of the questions they asked me. They were very friendly and gave me hot milk to drink. I had not eaten since early morning, so it was welcome.

I sat in a stupor of fatigue until two of the men prepared to leave, indicating that I should come with them. I understood that they were going to take me back with them to their village. I wanted to stay where I was, but they said it was not far. So I started off with them into the night again. It had begun to rain now, quite heavily, and the ground became sodden and slippery. We were climbing steeply and my legs trembled with fatigue as I staggered along behind my two guides. I soon reached the point where I could go no further and fell, exhausted, to the ground. The others stopped and held a consultation, but there was nothing to be done. After a rest, I dragged myself to my feet again and we went on, slower now.

I kept falling and resting every few hundred yards. The intervals became shorter. But the village was only a short distance now. Somehow we reached it at last. It was the very one that I had been in earlier in the day. I had had all that extra trouble unnecessarily. If only I had asked in the first place instead of taking the easy way. I crossed the ford again in a very weak state. Mounting the village street in the darkness was too much. The rain was pouring down now and the cobbles were slippery as a torrent of water flowed over them. I fell in a faint and lay there in the middle of the street.

When I revived some minutes later there was a conference going on round me. I was too tired to worry about them and just lay there. The cold water ran through my hair and down my back in a cool refreshing stream. I had already been soaked to the skin so I could not be wetter. The conference was to decide where to put me. People were apprehensive of being betrayed as having sheltered an escaped prisoner. One young man was speaking vehemently on the subject. Eventually it was all settled. I was to go in with him. I made a supreme effort and managed to follow him unaided to his house.

Despite my protests, he insisted on me occupying his bed. His house was a single-roomed shack on the edge of the village.

It contained a bed and a table. The bed consisted of wooden boards on trestles covered with carpet and some ancient and tattered blankets. There was a fire burning in the hearth. The man squatted there, blowing on the embers till they blazed up, while I took off my soaking clothes. He helped me when he saw my difficulties with my crippled arms. Soon I was in bed while he stayed on by the fire drying my clothes. His own were steaming on him. I went off into a deep sleep.

IV

Someone was shaking me. I came out of an empty void of unconsciousness. The room was lit only with the glow of embers in the fireplace, but through the window, grey streaks in the sky showed that dawn was near. My friend was standing by me. He indicated that it was time to go. He had sat by the fire all night long so that there was no danger of over-sleeping. I must be out of the village before dawn, before anyone could see where I had stayed.

I was tired and stiff but got up quickly and dressed. My clothes were warm and most of them were dry again. My boots were still soaking as they were much too precious to put by the fire. Soon I was ready. My friend escorted me outside and led me down the steep village street. We crossed the ford together before we spoke a word. Then he started to explain and showed me my route to the next village. It was light by now and I could see where it lay in the distance.

I was very grateful to him for the way he had risked his life to shelter me and for all his kindness. I wondered what I could give him. I thought of my mosquito net and pulled it out of my pocket. He was delighted with it. Just before we parted, I saw him looking appreciatively at my wrist-watch. I realised that it would be a priceless possession to a villager in the mountains. I took it off immediately. He was overcome by the magnitude of the gift. He handled the watch with awe.

It was time for him to go back now before anyone should be

about to see him. We parted and went our ways. I limped along the narrow goat trail round the mountain into the unknown again. The path was slippery after the rain and my boots collected huge cakes of sticky yellow mud. It was hard going and I was tired. The strain of the previous day had not worn off. I sat down at frequent intervals to rest.

Physically I was paying the price of over-exertion on the previous day. But I had learned that lesson; I should play my part in future. I realised that I had been wrong to expect God to help me if I would not help myself as far as I was able. Moreover, it had been moral cowardice that had prevented me from asking for shelter in that village in the first place. I determined to be different in future.

Although I was tired, my mind was at rest. I sauntered along peacefully. It was not far to the next village, perhaps two miles, but the state of the track and the steepness of the mountain combined with my own weakness to slow me up. It took me fully three hours. I paused on the steep slope above the village and wondered whether it was wise to go in. I prayed and felt immediate conviction that it would be all right. Down by the spring women were drawing water, and children were playing about the houses. I walked straight through. There were only about two dozen houses and there was the usual little white church in the middle. I went in here and knelt in thanksgiving. Some children came in with me and we sat there in the white coolness, they curious about the ragged stranger, I overwhelmed with gratitude for my freedom.

The inside of the church was simple and yet ornate. There were numerous ikons and the little altar was bright with brass and decorations. A gilded lamp hung from the roof and tapers drooped in front of niches where there were figures of the Virgin and local saints. The air was musty with the smell of stale incense. The children were getting restless. I smiled at them and we went out into the fresh mountain air.

They followed me down the twisting track through the village and shouted at the various village mongrels which snapped and barked at me. There were few grown-ups in sight. They were busy with their daily chores. On the outskirts of the village, I told the children to go on home and waved to them as we went our respective ways.

The track wound on round the mountain for another couple of miles. I went very slowly and sat and rested for long periods. When I came to the next village I was tempted to stay there. But this time my convinction was "Go on". I drank at the village spring and went into a little coffee house. Inside, I found a number of men playing cards, sipping Turkish coffee and playing backgammon. They were obviously curious, but in broad daylight they evidently considered it unwise to be seen fraternising with me.

I ordered coffee and was not allowed to pay for it. So I sat at a little table drinking it. At last someone came up and joined me. I invited him to play backgammon. We played a couple of games. I told him who I was. By this time others had unobtrusively joined us. They advised me to go on and get out of the village soon. I gathered that there was some danger, although I could not make out what it was. There were no Germans in the village but perhaps they expected a patrol. It seemed to tally with my inner conviction.

I slipped out and away down the winding track again. The coffee and conversation had freshened me and I moved faster now. I could see a large village in the distance, down in the valley. It was about four miles away. At the foot of the hill there was a wide stream. I forded it barefoot and sat drying my feet on the far side. I found myself on the edge of a road which ran north-west towards the lake and in the other direction led into this village.

A cart was approaching from the direction of the village. I considered hiding till it was past, but something told me it was all right and I sat and waited for it. There were two men with it and they stopped and came to talk to me. There were the usual questions, where from and where to. We chatted of the war, Albania and Crete. I knew they were all right; they were a couple of decent Greek soldiers and would be reliable advisers. I asked about the village just ahead. They told me that it was called Zagliveri and that I should not go into it in daylight. The Germans were frequently there. But it would be quite safe to go in after dark and there would be many who would be glad to give me shelter.

Soon they were on their way again and I slowly resumed my journey towards the village. I walked on the edge of the road where I could skip quickly away and hide if I saw any Germans coming. It was a long straight road of beaten earth lined with trees. I reached the outskirts of the village late in the afternoon. It was Sunday and, as in most other countries, it seemed to be the custom to promenade in best clothes. Streams of strollers were coming out towards me, mostly young folk in couples or little groups of three or four.

I greeted them as we passed and was followed by many a stare as I limped on, tired and sorefooted, but content in mind. I felt that I should stop by a bridge and sat down there expectantly. Within a few minutes a group of four young men in their best Sunday clothes had come up. They stopped to talk to me. Again there were the usual questions. Yes, I was an "Inglezi" fighter-pilot. I was going home. There was the usual laughter.

They looked round them surreptitiously. Seeing no one in sight, they told me to follow them. I was led down a side track to an empty building, half-ruined, which lay just on the edge of the village. Here we were free from spying eyes and possible interruptions. What were my plans? I was cautious at this point and asked what they advised. They were uniformly pessimistic. It was impossible to get out of the country these days, even for Greeks. They would all like to go and join the Greek Army in Egypt, but it was out of the question. The Germans had tightened their guard on all the possible routes. It was very dangerous.

They thought that my best plan would be to find somewhere safe to stay, perhaps with the shepherds in the hills, to await the return of the English. It could not be long now, they argued.

Again the words "Ayon Oros", the sacred mountain, were mentioned. Yes! That would be a good place to go; it was far away from everywhere. And maybe the monks would look after me. In the meantime, they would inquire about a bed for me for the night. Two of them went off to do this, leaving two others behind with me. We sat and chatted happily.

The evening drew on. I realised suddenly that I had not eaten since having breakfast with the shepherd on Saturday morning. This was Sunday evening. I was hungry. In the dusk, we saw four figures coming in our direction. I hid in case of trouble. The others waited, silent. The four came up and exchanged greetings. There were our two friends with two others. I stayed hidden until I was called out. The new-comers were rather cool in their greeting, but I felt it was all right. One was a little unfriendly. He asked in English what right I had to come and endanger the whole village. I replied that I felt it would be all right. This did not soothe him. He became hostile.

Suddenly I had the thought to mention the Houses at Salonika. His attitude underwent an immediate change when he heard that they were friends of mine. He had been one of their pupils and nothing was too good for a friend of Charles House. From then on all was well. The tension relaxed and my previous friends were obviously relieved and pleased. They had been silent and apprehensive throughout this conversation and the newcomers were clearly men of importance in the village.

It was dark by now and I was told to follow my English-speaking friend. The others were to leave me here. I said good-bye to them and thanked them for their help. It was made clear to me that I could only stay one night and that I must leave very early in the morning. It was not safe otherwise.

We stole silently into the village and turned down an alley. I was told to wait under a tree in the shadow while my guide went on. Soon he was back with someone else. This man was to be my host for the night. I was again reminded that I must be away before dawn and then I was left alone with my new friend.

A few yards away was his house. I went in with him. Inside,

I was greeted by his wife and two children. The room flickered by the light of a crude oil-lamp shaped like a sauce-boat burning olive oil through a drooping wick. A fire burned in the hearth and fresh wood was thrown on till it blazed high.

I was divested of my coat and seated on the floor with the others. The wife busied herself about the place while I chatted to the children. Soon there was a little table laid in the middle of the floor. It stood only a few inches high. We sat around it on the floor and a steaming bowl was brought in. It was soup. I only realised how hungry I was when I smelled it. It was followed by "peta", a flat wholemeal scone with spinach in it, made from dandelion leaves. The food tasted wonderful to my ravenous appetite.

Afterwards we sat round in the firelight. The lamp had gone out and oil was precious. We talked. I found that the family had lost their eldest boy, killed in Albania. The father had fought in the last war and in the Balkan War which ended in 1923. He had been twice wounded. I showed them my wounded right arm swathed in bandages. It struck me that it must be pretty foul inside now after two days without dressing. The wife wept over it and started to take the bandage off. I demurred, thinking it was hardly the time to expose a festering wound, immediately after dinner. But she insisted. The bandage was unwound and I was astounded to find no trace of pus. I could hardly believe my eyes. The wound had been discharging steadily for ten months, yet now it looked firm and healthy. It must have closed as I escaped, healed with my headache and fever on that first memorable evening. Yet another miracle.

The good wife also said she would mend my tattered trousers. They hung in rags about my legs; the mountain thorns and shepherds' dogs had not been kind to them. I was finding it very hard to stay awake. They noticed this and hustled me off to bed upstairs. I had it all to myself — the usual wooden boards covered with blankets and rugs. I undressed, helped by my host, and gave him my trousers for mending. As soon as I lay down I was asleep.

VIII

MACEDONIA – THE HIGH ROAD

I

It was still dark when I was awakened. I dragged myself out of
the depths of deep sleep. It was difficult to realise where I was
in the darkness. At first I thought I was at home. Then, slowly,
the mists dissolved and time became something to reckon with
again. My host was standing by me with my trousers.

He helped me to dress and we went downstairs where his
wife was brewing coffee in the glowing charcoal of last night's
fire. It was Turkish coffee, thick and sweet in a little cup with a
glass of cold water. I thanked them profusely in a variety of
languages. My host was to show me the road out of the village
and we walked off quietly together in the dark grey dawn. He
walked fifty paces ahead so as to avoid any identification in
case we were caught. I strolled along, pretending not to know
him, but there were few people about so early in the morning.
Occasional shadowy figures passed by in the opposite direction.

We reached the edge of the village and the path led on into
the open country. My host stopped and I came up to him and
thanked him again. I wanted to give him something and
fumbled in my pocket. I had 4,000 drachma in notes when I
started. I pulled out a note for 1,000 and pressed it into his
hand. He demurred but I insisted, saying that it was for the
children. Eventually he accepted it and we parted.

I strolled on in the gathering light. The path led up a long
valley, through orchards and olive groves. At the head of the
valley there was some marshy ground and then the path climbed
through scrub and wild olive trees up the stony side of the

mountain again. I rested frequently in the shade. The sun was up now and it was becoming warmer. The path dwindled until it was scarcely discernible among the maze of goat tracks. I crossed a ridge and sauntered on in the warm afternoon. There was no sign of habitation or human beings.

Crossing another ridge, I found myself looking out over a broad valley. A large river ran down the middle between cultivated fields. Beyond, the hills rose again in serried ranks to the horizon. About halfway down the hill to the river, I came upon a little white house standing sentinel over the fields below. Two women stood in the door, gazing curiously at me as I approached. I asked for water. They hastened to bring me some from an earthenware jar in the shade. We chatted. There were the usual questions and answers — who I was, where I was from, where I was going. I asked them, "Pou ine Ayon Oros?" Which way to the sacred mountain? They looked at each other almost as if sharing some secret which they could not divulge. Then they pointed to a distant peak. That was not the mountain. It was five or six days' march beyond. But my direction had been sound. I was still heading for the monasteries.

I went on and sat for a time by the river, watching the swollen stream sweeping steadily past between its tree-lined banks. Walking slowly upstream, looking for a possible crossing, I came upon a man ploughing. He must have been a rich farmer, because he drove a wooden plough behind two bullocks. The red earth twisted away from the ploughshare and the crows gathered behind as the team strained and grunted in the hot afternoon sun. He was a young man and stopped to talk to me. He had fought in Albania and still wore his army battle-dress trousers. He was very friendly. Yes, Ayon Oros would be a good place for me. Many English had been there before. But he was gloomy about my prospects of getting out of the country. It would be quite impossible. He himself had tried to escape to join the Greek Army in the Middle East, but the German net had grown tighter of late. It was difficult even for Greeks to be smuggled out of the country. It was the same story which

I had heard before.

He told me there was a ford across the river a little higher up by a mill and I walked on slowly till I came to it. The river was about fifty yards wide here and ran fast and shallow across the stones. As I sat, taking off my boots and socks, I was startled to find someone beside me. He had appeared without a sound through the bushes. We looked at each other guardedly. I was reassured. He was obviously a Greek soldier, in tattered battle-dress. I explained myself and he too was reassured. As I prepared to enter the water, I noticed that he had only taken one boot off. I wondered how he was going to cross the stream. To my astonishment, he entered the water hopping on his one bare foot and hopped his way across the fifty yards of rushing water and sharp stones to the far bank. As I picked my way tenderly across, I found it hard to retain my balance on the slippery stones which bruised and cut my soft feet. Evidently his method called for considerable acclimatisation. I learned that it was typical Greek Army practice and it certainly saved time and trouble if you were sufficiently tough.

We walked on together. Again I asked about Ayon Oros, the mystery mountain. I noticed him look curiously at me, but he seemed reassured and said that he thought that it was the best place for me to go. But he too was very doubtful of my chances of getting away. He also had tried and failed.

We came to a village called Marathousa and I bade him farewell. I had a hunch to seek out someone here and inquired from some children if there were any English. No, there were no English but there had been some several months ago. They would not tell me where they had stayed and evaded my questions. Perhaps they did not understand. I still felt that there was something to follow up here and went to a house in the middle of the village. I walked up to the door and knocked firmly on it. There were footsteps inside. The door opened and I said in English, "I am an English officer. Please, can you help me?"

"How did you know where to come?" the man replied in

English. He quickly pulled me inside out of sight. I found myself in a little room with three children and a man and his wife. The man was emaciated and hollow-eyed in tattered clothing. His wife was a terrible sight; she was about to have a child and her appearance contrasted strangely with her sunken cheeks and thin arms. The children looked healthier. Evidently they had what food there was. They gathered round me, wide-eyed.

I explained myself in detail, who I was, where I had come from, where I hoped to go. My friend could not understand how it was I had chanced upon his house without human direction. It was he who had helped to house and feed a number of escaped British troops some months earlier. They had remained with him for weeks, but he had heard that, later, they had been unsuccessful in their attempts and were still in the country or recaptured.

He advised me very strongly against going to Ayon Oros. He said he had heard from travellers that the monks were starving and that the Germans raided the monasteries frequently by boat to check up on them as they were suspected of having housed escaped British prisoners. He described the five days' march down the long finger of land to the sacred mountain. There was no road or reasonable track. Only a mountaineer could make the journey safely. I had no provisions to last me for five days' march through uninhabited country, and I was in no shape for mountain climbing. I pondered while he described the difficulties.

Instead, he recommended me to go back on my tracks slightly and head south-west to Moudania. This small port on the Gulf of Salonika at the base of the Kassandhra Peninsula was a centre for smugglers operating the black market between Salonika and the islands. Perhaps I could persuade the smugglers to take me with them to the islands, and then find some other means to reach the Turkish mainland. I decided to take his advice. It seemed as if I had not met him for nothing, and the reason might be to save me a long and arduous trek.

Meanwhile, his wife was busy with her bowl and a little flour

134

and some dandelion leaves collected by the children from the hillside. She was making peta. It was the only food they had and they had no idea where the next meal would come from. As I prepared to leave they tried to press half of it on me. It was all they could do and they were nearly in tears to have to send me on my way unaided. I hastily assured them that I was all right, and was able to persuade them to keep the precious food for themselves. As I left, I remembered my vitamin tablets and pulled them out of my pocket. The precious vitamins would be life-saving to this family and the man accepted them gladly for his children. We said good-bye and I set my face to the south-west.

The man had given me the name of a friend in a nearby village who, he said, would be able to shelter me for the night. It was about two hours' march away and the evening shadows lengthened as I plodded along the winding track through scrub and ravine, across streams and through tiny patches of cultivation. He had advised me not to go into the village in daylight so as to avoid compromising his friend in case there were Germans about. It was getting dark as I reached the village and I found a shepherd coming in from the hills for the night.

I asked him, "Pou ine Kalivas?" My unsuspecting host was a miller called Kalivas. The shepherd led me to his mill in the dusk. I knocked on the door; after some delay it was opened and I was dragged quickly inside. Kalivas lived with his wife in a little room at the back of the mill. I explained myself as usual, this time in French of which he spoke a little. He too was thin and wasted, but was anxious to help me. His wife made me up a couch in the room with them. I was very tired. There was nothing to eat and there was no light, so there was little inducement to prolong our halting conversation. They helped me off with my boots and I fell back into a deep sleep.

II

It was raining in the morning and the mists hung on the

135

mountain slopes above the village. I was up and away shortly after dawn before the place was astir. No one was in sight as I slipped out of the mill and away on the winding mountain track leading to the south-west. The track was slippery and the mud heavy on my boots and I was tired. After a couple of hours I had only covered a few miles. The rain fell steadily and I was wet and sweating.

I came upon a village tucked away in a steep gully. It was called Geroplatanos. The houses clung to the hillside like limpets on a boulder. One of them was a coffee house. Inside the steaming window I could see people sitting at tables, sipping coffee. They looked friendly and I was tired and lonely. I walked boldly in.

Conversation died away as everyone stared at me. I had a moment's qualm. Would they be friends or foes? Perhaps there was a German patrol here. But my mind was quickly reassured. I greeted the assembled company and explained myself in the usual way. They could not doubt that I was genuinely English. The Germans sometimes sent spies round as a trick to try to discover how escaped prisoners were being helped. But my identity was in no doubt; my height and my helpless arms told their own tale.

I sat down and a little group gathered round me, plying me with questions. The stout proprietress came forward with coffee and soon she bustled in with an unheard-of gift for me —a hard-boiled egg. Then there was bread and olives. I had a wonderful meal, surrounded by friendship and the spirit which was so characteristic of these mountain folk. They were ragged, unshaven, fierce-looking and excitable, but the greatest-hearted people I had met and I loved them.

We talked of many things; of the war, of home, of the future. The war had hit this country harder than any other in Europe with the possible exception of Poland. The Albanian campaign had been a glorious chapter in the history of freedom, but the Greek victories had not been bought cheaply; their casualties had been heavy. Then there had been the disastrous

days of the retreat before the Germans. And now the occupation was costing them a fantastic price in famine and death.
Worst of all, perhaps, the sufferings of a tortured people were
to be mobilised by the Communists and turned into hatreds
which would still further consume the country with their fires.

It was fortunate, perhaps, that the sombre view of the future
was hidden. Everyone in Greece expected that the country
would be liberated by a great Allied thrust into the Balkans
during the summer of 1942. Few were aware of the length of
time required to train and deploy a great army. Most people
expected the whole enormous resources of the United States
to be available immediately after Pearl Harbour.

Everyone I met in Greece at that time was a devoted friend
of Britain. We had come to their aid at a time when our own
fortunes were at a low ebb. We had bled with them; we would
surely liberate them. They looked to Britain and America, not
only for the force which would eventually set them free again,
but also for the moral strength and way of life which would
replace the twisted politics and violent vendettas of the old
régime. The dictatorship of Metaxas had not been as bad as
some perhaps, but it had been a dictatorship nevertheless, with
its secret police and all the repression of opposition which that
implies. In a true democracy opposition is not repressed, it is
outvoted. Greece's greatest need, then as now, was to be shown
how the hatred could be healed instead of exploited — how
people could unite together with a new spirit — how the home
of freedom could become free again. It was one of the saddest
features of post-war Europe that the free world failed to meet
this need, and so allowed our gallant Greek friends to be still
further tortured by the horrors of internal war.

My friends were devoted admirers of Mr. Churchill. He symbolised for them the strength and spirit of Britain at that time.
They said to me, "If you manage to reach home, tell Mr.
Churchill that we are here and that, no matter how long it
takes, he will find us still here fighting when the British come
again." The outrageous optimism and gallantry of these simple

137

mountain people made me gasp with admiration. Unthinkingly, I agreed. "Yes, I will tell Mr. Churchill." I little thought how that promise, lightly given but seriously received, would be fulfilled in the future. It seemed a far cry from the mountains of Macedonia to No. 10 Downing Street. But after my return home I did in fact lunch with the then Prime Minister and Mrs. Churchill, and told them my fantastic tale, reminiscent in some ways of Mr. Churchill's own escape during the South African War. They were deeply moved and later, of course, they were to play a dramatic role in trying to solve Greece's post-war troubles. Who but Mr. Churchill would have flown to Athens to address the masses gathered in Constitution Square to hear him in those dangerous days of 1944?

We sat for hours in the coffee-house sipping "ersatz" coffee and talking. There was a doctor present, the only professional man for many miles around, called Dr. Kaltsas. He spoke fluent French and it was a pleasure to be able to converse freely with him. Before I left, I suddenly remembered the medicines which I was carrying and presented them to him. He had not seen aspirin or quinine for months, and the sulphanilamides were priceless in a country where medical supplies could not be bought. He told me he had had the heartbreaking task of treating sick people without the means to make them well. I knew that my drugs had been a godsend.

As I left, the doctor pressed me to accept money for the medicines. I felt it wrong to accept when his need seemed so much greater than mine. He said, "You are crazy. You will never escape from Greece without money." I told him I believed that God would continue to provide for me. He was incredulous, but I was firm, and we parted with the whole village gathered to speed me on my way. I hated to leave them but I had a long road to travel.

The rain had stopped by now and the clouds were breaking. Shafts of sunlight were slashing swords, piercing the stormy sky and tearing the clouds asunder. Wisps of mist were still hanging to the trees on the mountain slopes, and the interplay

138

of light and shade on the rain-freshened leaves was exhilarating. All the scents latent in the spring soil had been released by the rain, and the anemones glinted like stars beside the trail.

An old man came with me to show me the road. He strode with the long, steady stride of the mountaineer and his pig-skin sandals collected far less mud than my army boots. We were climbing steadily over the mountain range and I would lag behind till we were separated by several hundred yards. At this, he would stop and wait for me to catch him up, smiling a little, happy that his old bones were still more than a match for me. We went on like this until we crossed the ridge and could see a village in the distance on the farther side. I had to go there and then away beyond into the distant hills. I thanked him and we parted and I watched his long, loping stride carrying him swiftly from boulder to boulder across the rough stony ground as he headed for home.

I rested for some time, watching the cloud shadows flit across the scene and scenting the fragrant breezes which blew off the hills. Then it was time to go and I strolled on gently along the rough goat track leading to the village.

It was not long before I came upon a man with a donkey. The donkey was carrying an enormous load of firewood. The man was another young Greek soldier, and like so many of them was still wearing his army trousers. We quickly made friends and he told me about Albania and described his efforts to get out of the country to join the Greek Army in Egypt. He warned me that there were Germans in the village ahead. I would have blundered straight into them. We left the goat track just above the village and I followed him in and out of gullies and by circuitous paths so that we avoided it.

The place was called Ayo Prodromos. It lay on the main road between Salonika and Poligyros. We came upon the road suddenly through the scrub. I shrank back into hiding behind a boulder. There was a lorry driving up the road and lorries meant Germans. It stopped some distance away and figures got out and went into a house on the outskirts of the village. My friend beckoned to me and I walked quickly across the road and away on the other side through the bushes. Here he left me, pointing in the direction which I had to go. I strode on, putting as much distance as possible between me and the village and keeping out of sight of the road.

I was climbing again and became very tired. The afternoon sun had broken through and it was very hot. I found myself unable to walk more than two hundred paces or so without resting. I would set myself a mark on the hill and plod steadily up to it. When I reached it, I would collapse on the ground and rest. Then I would repeat the performance.

Very slowly I mounted the hill. I was extremely thirsty and there was no water. It seemed ages before I came upon a track again. This led upwards but not quite so steeply and I was able to make a better pace. Across a ridge, I came upon a spring by the side of the road. There was a stone trough with water pouring into it from a little stream. I sank on my knees beside it and plunged my face into the water. It was ice cold and exquisitely fresh and clear.

As I rested there, I saw that it was evening and that it would soon be dark. An old man approached, leading a herd of goats. We greeted each other and walked on slowly together. I asked him how far the village was. It was quite close. I asked if there were any Germans there. No, there were no Germans. I hoped that he would invite me to his home, but he was evidently afraid to do this. However, he told me that there was a hotel here, a rare occurrence for a mountain village in Greece. I asked him to direct me to it and we came into the village in the gloaming together. We stopped beside a largish white stone house. It looked clean and cool and its windows looked out towards the valley far below.

I knocked on the door. It was opened cautiously a few inches and I was scanned carefully by an old woman with a wrinkled, weather-beaten face and kind eyes. She seemed satisfied and welcomed me in. Soon I was surrounded by the household, all women. They fussed over me and wept over my crippled arms.

I was very tired and could hardly keep my eyes open. They showed me to an upstairs room, beautifully clean with a bare, wooden floor and a bedstead in the corner. Two or three women were bustling around, putting a mattress and sheets and a quilt on the bed. They helped me off with my coat and left me alone. In a few minutes I was in bed and asleep.

III

I must have slept far into the next day. I was wakened by a policeman shaking me. I sat up and noticed that it was snowing heavily outside. You could not see more than a few yards beyond the windows. The policeman was a Greek and wanted to see my papers. I smiled at him and said that I had none. He smiled back and said that I must have some. So I pointed to the identity discs hanging round my neck and said: "These are my papers." He was delighted to find that he could honestly record that I had papers. He said: "They will be in order for you to travel here?" I said: "Yes, they will be in order for me to travel anywhere." He said: "They will be fully recognised by the Germans?" I said: "Yes, they will be fully recognised by the Germans." He was entranced. We laughed heartily together.

He told me that the village was called Vavdos. It was visited by German patrols and it would not be safe for me to stay more than twenty-four hours. I asked him if I might stay till the following day in view of the snow. He agreed, provided that I got away early in the morning. So I settled down to spend a wonderful day in bed, most of the time asleep. My five days of steady walking had hardened my muscles, but my illness and the long months in hospital had left me with very little stamina. It was wonderful to be given a day like this to rest and prepare for the next stage. I read my little New Testament, amazed at the fresh truth that struck me on every page, recognising my own experiences of the past weeks and learning from them and the mistakes which I had made.

I recognised by now that, provided I acted boldly in faith,

following my highest conviction and doing the best I knew, God would never let it come to any serious harm and the experience would always be used in some miraculous way to further His plan. I only went wrong when I doubted or allowed fears or indulgences or pride and self-will to rule my decisions. This time of rest had been given me to take stock of my position as well as to rest my bones.

The old ladies who ran the hotel visited me from time to time to see that I was all right. They were in tears because they had no food to offer me. They had none themselves. They hoped to get some bread on the following day. I was only concerned because they were. I did not feel hungry or distressed at the lack of food. I was content just to lie peacefully and read and rest.

In the afternoon, I gave myself the luxury of a shave. I sent for a barber and a young man came, accompanied by half the village, to shave me. The room was crowded with enthusiastic spectators as he worked hard to produce a lather from a scrap of very inferior soap and a filthy old brush. Soon he was at work removing the five days' growth of beard with deft hands. I felt clean and refreshed and had a good chat with the crowd. I rummaged about among my things and found a stick of shaving soap. I cut it in half and gave the barber half. There were exclamations of delight from all around. The soap was English and they had never seen such soap before. It was white and it lathered so quickly. I could come back for free shaves in that village for the rest of my days. Somehow we persuaded the crowd to leave and I settled down to rest again in peace.

The following morning I woke to find a clear sky and no trace of snow. The view was superb. Looking out of the window there was a drop of several thousand feet down to the road which I had crossed the day before. On the other side of the valley the mountains rose in jagged ridges to the distant peak of Kissos Khortiates. The air was clear as you only find it in mountain countries. It was like the west of Scotland on a June day. You could see a hundred miles, and every detail of the mountain slopes stood out sharp and clear.

A young boy appeared with a bowl of water and helped me to wash and dress. I kissed the old ladies farewell and they wept again to see me go, making me promise to return. "Soon the English will be here." Alas for the years which would pass before that came true!

I walked off down the sunlit street, waving to them and smiling a greeting at the occasional passer-by. Soon I was out on the hillside again, winding round the steep shoulders of the mountian, climbing steadily to still another ridge. I was fresh and rested, and moved steadily along. I had soon crossed the ridge and started to make the long slow descent to the sea.

I kept clear of villages or passed quickly through them on my way down. I was making good time downhill and my rest at Vavdos had given me new determination and energy. About midday I found myself within two hours' march of Nea Moudania. I was coming to the cultivated coastal belt, and fields of growing corn became more numerous.

In a dried river-bed I found three men collecting weeds to eat. They were picking dandelions for spinach. They were obviously ex-army men and I stopped and chatted with them. I asked them if there were any Germans in Moudania. To my dismay, they said that there were. The smugglers' boats could no longer ply there and it would be unsafe to go in. I was at a loss to know what to do next. But I felt that my encounter with those men had some purpose, so I asked them where they recommended me to go. They replied without hesitation. I should go to Ayo Nikolaos at the base of the middle finger of the Sithonia peninsula. There I would find some smugglers who might take me to the islands. After that I should have to take my chance of reaching the Turkish coast.

I left them and walked a little way in the direction they had indicated. Then I sat down and reviewed the position carefully. I prayed to be shown the right way. It seemed very clear to me that it would be wrong to compromise the Greeks by trying to go into Moudania, knowing that there were Germans there. So

I must face the long trail to Ayo Nikolaos. I was relieved to have my mind clarified, and set off again with renewed determination in a southerly direction. I had no idea what the future held in store. It was enough for me to know that to-day was good and the road straight ahead.

IV

For some miles the track wound over undulating country, steadily losing height as it approached the sea. Coming over the crest of one small hill I saw a substantial white stone farmhouse just ahead. It was almost like an English farm with outhouses and cottages. Some men were working in the yard and a dog barked as I approached.

I called out to them as I got nearer, "Kali mera" — good morning. They came out to greet me and we sat by the wayside chatting for some time. I suddenly realised that I was hungry and, almost with the thought, came the offer of food. A woman came out from the farmhouse carrying a piece of bread and some black olives wrapped in a cloth. I accepted them gratefully and munched as we talked. Children came round too, and soon I was the centre of a friendly and curious little group. We talked on for an hour or so, oblivious of time or the necessity to go anywhere or do anything. Then I felt I should be moving on, so I asked them where they advised me to go. They confirmed what my earlier friends had told me: I should go to Ayo Nikolaos.

I set off again, promising to return some day. Coming to a river, I had a moment of difficulty to know where to cross. I walked impatiently up the bank, hoping to find some obvious crossing. Then came the thought, "You can cross here." Although the river was wide and looked deep, I took off my boots and waded barefoot into the stream. The water came just above my knees but never higher, and I walked slowly across, balancing on the big slippery stones.

The trail led on through a wooded belt and came out into

cultivated fields near a village. I paused for direction again and then moved on round the outskirts of the village, feeling that it would be unwise to venture in during daylight. By this time it was early evening and I was pleasantly weary. I sat down to rest by some bushes and dozed for a while.

When I woke, a man was standing by me. He was carrying a huge basket filled with kitchenware. He appeared to be a travelling salesman. A young man, like most of the others, he was wearing army battledress trousers and had fought in Albania. When he heard that I was "Inglezi" he embraced me and pulled a filthy package wrapped in cloth from his pocket. Unwrapping it, a cream cheese was disclosed. Once white, it now bore many stains, including some bright blue colouring off the cloth in which it was wrapped. However, it was more valuable than gold in a country where gold could not help you to eat. He cut off a large chunk and gave it to me. I accepted it gratefully and we parted company. His trail would lead him to Salonika, while mine lay out into the unknown.

I strolled on towards the coast while the shadows lengthened. I was walking through olive groves now, and the trees cast their long shadows across the trail. Coming over the crest of a little hill I caught a glimpse of a large white farmhouse lying well back off the trail among orchards. It was not yet dusk, but I had a strong feeling that I should go and visit this house and perhaps stay the night there. Unsure whether this was right or merely wishful, I sat for some time by the roadside. Gradually conviction grew and I walked off confidently towards the house.

It was a fine farmhouse, bigger than any I had seen so far. It stood by itself among beautiful orchards and I walked boldly up to the front door and knocked. I heard movement within and had the sense of being inspected through the windows. But I restrained my curiosity and waited patiently, facing the door. In a few moments it opened an inch or two and a man looked me over carefully. He spoke to me in rapid Greek which I could not understand.

All I thought to say was, "I am an English fighter-pilot." I

145

repeated it in French and, to my delight, he answered in French which was just about as understandable as my own.

He invited me in and I was ushered into a sitting-room where three other men were seated. They all questioned me at once, a little suspiciously. They wanted me to produce papers to show who I was. I pulled out a letter I had had from my mother which I had treasured in an inside pocket. The envelope was, of course, addressed to me through the Red Cross. It was closely inspected by everybody and seemed to satisfy them. They became more friendly. I answered all their questions immediately and fully; how I was captured, where my home was, where I had been prisoner, when I had escaped.

When it came to the question, "Where are you going?" I explained that I had no particular reason for going anywhere except that ultimately I hoped to reach home. We laughed together. Then I told them that I had been advised to go to Ayon Oros, then to Nea Moudania and now to Ayo Nikolaos. The men looked at each other.

I added that I felt sure that my journey had so far been controlled by God and that I was sure it would continue to lead me to some purpose or end which I could not foresee, but which was the one intended for me. The men looked at each other again in surprise, almost consternation. There was rapid conversation in Greek.

Then my host turned to me and said, "You will stay with us to-night and to-morrow I will take you to join some of your friends." I asked him what he meant and he explained that Derek Scott and the two Australian medical orderlies, who had escaped from Salonika some weeks before me, had come to that very house for shelter and aid.

I was both astounded and delighted to hear that I should be seeing my friend Derek Scott again so soon and so unexpectedly. Of all the places in Greece, to have chosen the same house to visit was certainly remarkable. I had no idea which direction Derek would go from Salonika. He might have gone anywhere, yet here we were, knocking on the same door within a few days of each other. I was grateful as I realised again the reason I had come in — the silent thought which had caused me so many times to choose the right place and the right person.

Soon I was led upstairs to a beautiful, clean bedroom. It was simply furnished. There was a typical Greek bed, wooden boards on trestles, with a carpet and rugs on top of it for bed-clothes. I was very tired. My host explained that he wanted me to remain up there until we should leave together the following evening after dark. I was to keep out of sight of everybody and he would bring my food up personally. I thanked him and he left me alone. I knelt by the bed and thanked God for bringing me there. Then I slept soundly for many hours.

During the following day I lay, resting peacefully, occasion-ally reading in my little New Testament. At midday I was brought up a great delicacy, a bowl of hot soup. I had expected to have to subsist on the piece of bread and cheese which were still in my pocket from the previous day. The soup was followed by a dish of beautifully cooked rice with some chicken in it. I feasted royally.

At the end of the long peaceful day, the dusk drew in and I prepared to leave. I dressed and put on my boots once more. About half an hour after dark my host appeared, dressed for the road, and we slipped through the house and out on to the trail.

The evening air was fresh, and scented with all the flavours of the day. There was the fresh feel of falling dew and the stars twinkled in a cloudless sky. For the most part we walked in silence, picking our way in single file along the narrow trail. I was rested after my stay at the farm and had no difficulty in keeping up with my guide. His slow stride was typical of moun-tain folk the world over. I kept in step with him and we made good time over the rough track.

After a couple of hours, we had reached our destination. I could hear the waves breaking on a beach close by. We left the track and climbed through some pine-trees, richly scented, to a small white villa standing high above the shore. My guide knocked at the door and it was opened by an old man, carrying a flickering oil-lamp. His wrinkled face lit up when he saw us and I was welcomed like a son. They showed me a bed. It was a proper one with springs and a mattress and good blankets. It was not long before I was fast asleep again.

V

When I woke in the morning, I found that my guide had left. The old man had insructions to tell me to keep out of the house during the day. So I left him and headed up the hillside for a short distance. I found a spring of fresh water and settled down among some bushes near it. The sun was shining from a cloudless sky and it was pleasant sitting there in the shade.

I was surrounded by the typical scrub and small trees which cover so many of the mountain slopes in this part of the country. Below me lay a patch of pines with the white villa perched among them. Below and beyond stretched white sands, washed by the clear blue Aegean. Away out on my right reached the long finger of Kassandhra, running south from Nea Moudania. Beyond it, out of sight, lay the Gulf of Salonika and far in the distance rose the great mountain ranges around Olympus, capped with snow. On the left, the second peninsula of Sithonia, a long low reach of hills, stretched southwards from Ayo Nikolaos. In the bay, a few fishing-boats were sailing far out and the sun caught their sails and sparkled on the water round them. It was an exquisite scene and I gazed spellbound for many hours while the warm breeze slipped fragrantly by.

Occasionally I saw people pass on the road below the villa but no one came up the hill or approached the house. In the evening, I made my way down the hill and knocked on the door. The old man let me in and had some "ersatz" coffee, brewed by the fireside, ready for me. We broke bread together, tearing the remains of my loaf apart and munching it appreciatively.

Later, there was a knock at the door. I prepared to hide but

148

was reassured by the old man. My guides had come to take me on the next stage. Two men came in and we rapidly made friends with each other. After smoking a cigarette they were ready to go and we set off in the dusk together.

This time the trail led away from the sea and we walked slowly, one behind the other. We came to a collection of tents. They were black and inhabited by shepherds from the mountains. These were a special race with long black beards and black cloaks. They would spend the winter with their flocks in the low country and then, as the summer advanced, they would head for the high mountains on the Bulgarian border which were their real home. They were a nomad people and had come and gone like this for centuries.

Some of them were standing by the trail as we went past. There was enough light to distinguish them quite clearly. I was warned not to say anything to anyone but to walk quietly past. Among the black-bearded figures was one of slighter build. He had no cloak and looked suspiciously like a British soldier. However, I obeyed my instructions and passed within a few yards of him without saying a word. We looked curiously at each other and the glance was our only link as we passed in the night, far from home.

My guides told me that there were a few of our men who had escaped from the Germans but were unable to get out of the country. They were living with these nomad bands of shepherds, supported by them and fitting into their slow routine. When the weather was warmer, they would take to the road again.

I struck me that it might be my lot to live like this for a time. I laughed to picture what my friends would think of me; looking after sheep or goats would be quite a change after a squadron of Hurricanes. But I was prepared for anything. Whatever happened, life could not fail to remain a high adventure.

IX

ORMELIA

I

After a couple of hours we approached a village. It was called Ormelia and it lay peacefully among the mountains which stretched up behind it, range after range to the north.

In the outskirts, we stopped by a little house. One of my guides went in to make sure that everything was all right. Soon he beckoned us to come in too. We found ourselves in a tiny room, crowded with people. There was my guide's wife and three small children, another man's wife and various friends. Suddenly I saw my friend Derek Scott standing in the corner smiling all over his face. We greeted each other almost casually as if it was only natural that we should be meeting like this in the house of some friends.

With him was a large young man with the unmistakable look of the British regular soldier. He was introduced to me as Harry Brown and he smiled as we shook hands. "I am so glad you have arrived, sir," he said. He explained that word had come through that I was on my way and Derek and he had been summoned from their hiding-place in the hills to come down to meet me and take me back with them. I gathered from Harry and Derek that they were a party of eight up there. The medical orderlies who had escaped with Derek had parted company with him to return to Salonika where they were later recaptured.

It was stuffy in the little room as we sat and reminisced. It was a relief to be able to talk English again. Harry's home was in Bristol and he had a slow West-country drawl. He had been in the British Army, in the artillery, for several years before the war, serving in Palestine and the Middle East. Captured in Crete, he had made several attempts to escape. He had finally succeeded in jumping off the train which was carrying him from Salonika to Belgrade en route for Germany. He and the others had teamed up together and had made many attempts to cross to Turkey.

He told me that they had traversed the long and arduous trail down the Ayon Oros Peninsula to Mount Athos on five separate occasions in the hope that the monks would be able to help them to get away. Each time they had had to come all the way back again — a week's march in each direction — across the jagged peaks and twisting mountain trails. They had completely worn through their army boots and had been forced to wear Greek peasant sandals made from the skin of wild boar. For a time during the winter they had had to go bare-footed for lack of anything to wear. Their clothes were in rags, torn by the tough mountain thorn. In the autumn they had all caught malaria, some very badly. One Australian sergeant was so bad that he had to be carried in to a neighbouring village to hand himself over to the Germans. I remembered meeting him in the prison camp at Salonika as he slowly recuperated.

Harry and his friends had walked many hundreds of miles through the mountains of Macedonia during the nine or ten months since their escape. During the winter, they had built themselves a stone hut up in the hills near this village of Ormelia. They had lived there for several months, fed by the faithful village folk whenever there was food to be had. Sometimes they had gone for days without eating anything.

I marvelled at their endurance and at the resourcefulness of the ordinary man faced with a threat to his liberty. There was nothing that they would not do to remain free and no exertion or hardship too great for them when the goal was home. Simple things, home and freedom, they are deep-seated in the fabric of our living.

Harry seemed to have been one of the leaders of the party.

151

He was only a youngster but had the initiative, resourcefulness and steady judgement which marked him as an outstanding fellow. Nevertheless, he was relieved at my arrival and was clearly hoping to hand over responsibility for the party to me.

By contrast my young and hare-brained friend, Derek Scott, looked like an overgrown schoolboy. He was unshaven and his curly hair was tousled and standing up like a mop on his head. He had only been out of prison about two weeks, yet he looked more disreputable than Harry who had been out for ten months. He was full of impatience to do something, whatever it might be. He found waiting very difficult. But his enthusiasm and cheerfulness were a tonic at any time. I felt very grateful to have been brought so amazingly into touch with him like this.

Our friends were clustered all round us as we talked and there was a continual background noise of Greek chatter. I noticed the children climb quietly to bed in a corner of the room and go to sleep as though nothing was happening. The firelight flickered on their young faces as they lay, unconscious of the turmoil and trouble in the world around them.

Soon we were led out of the house again and up the narrow village street, stumbling over the cobbles, to another house where we were to dine. We were introduced to our hostess, the wife of one of the crowd we had met earlier. They had prepared a special feast for us. There was soup and chicken, great delicacies, and Derek and Harry and I were ravenously hungry. We ate to our hearts' content and laughed uproariously. It seemed so funny to be eating proper food again. Besides, we had eaten so much that our bellies were stretched and we were in that hilarious mood which follows over-eating.

After dinner there was a knock on the door and two men came in who were to guide us back up to our hiding-place in the mountains and also help carry the provisions for the next few days. There was a sack with some beans, some loaves of bread and a bag of olives. There was also a large package of tobacco. There were many expressions of goodwill as we set off for the long trek up into the hills. It appeared that our host was mayor of the village, or at least its leading and most prosperous citizen. His name was Agapitos Agapitos. We were to see more of him later.

We walked in silence until we were well clear of the village, then we chatted again among ourselves as we walked in single file behind our guides. The guides were cousins. One was a black-haired giant called Mitsios. He spoke only Greek so our conversation was limited. He carried the sack of provisions slung lightly over his shoulder. Behind him came his cousin Alekko. More slightly built, he was better educated and spoke some French. He seemed to be some relative of Agapitos and it had been his house to which we had been first taken.

Before long we came to a river. It was about twenty yards across and the stream flowed fast over large rocks. It was fairly deep at this point and wading in the dark would be a hazardous occupation. But there was a tree-trunk felled across the stream nearby and we elected to cross on it. It was slippery and not very stable. Unable to use my arms, I walked off on the swaying trunk hopefully. Mitsios was in front of me casting an anxious eye backwards to see how I was getting on. Near the far side, I slipped and would have fallen if he had not reached quickly back to grasp me. He pulled me over the remaining section, one enormous hand gripping my coat. The others crossed without incident and we went on up the mountainside.

The trail led steeply upwards over rocks and small streams, round the side of gullies, climbing steadily. I became very tired and had difficulty in keeping up. Mitsios' ever-watchful eye noticed this and he slackened his pace. Harry Brown was behind me, giving me a helping hand from time to time. I was surrounded by friends and uplifted and borne along by their caring. Nevertheless, it seemed ages before Mitsios announced that we were nearly there. We made the last climb to the hiding-place at a quicker pace. Suddenly, through the scrub and young trees, I caught sight of the glimmer of a fire. Voices called in greeting. We had arrived.

Our hiding-place was about three hours' march away from the village. It had taken us about four hours in the darkness. It lay high up on the slopes of the first range of mountains behind Ormelia, about 2,000 feet above sea-level. Our camp was carved out of the thick brushwood on the side of a gully. It consisted of a little circular clearing about ten paces across. In the middle of this was dug a pit where the wood fire burned continuously day and night, kept replenished from a pile of wood nearby. A few yards away in the thick scrub, another small clearing had been cut about six yards long by three yards wide. The trees were left at the corners and along the sides, forming a natural wall which had been reinforced with branches cut from neighbouring trees. The roof was brushwood supported on long poles and partly covered over with a tarpaulin which was not quite big enough to cover the entire surface. The front was open, facing downhill through the trees. A visitor could not see the shelter until he got within a few paces of it.

Where shepherds watched their flocks by night, the common practice was to build a huge bonfire beside the stockade in which the sheep or goats were tethered. The shepherds' fires twinkled on every hillside so ours would not be an unusual feature. And we could rely on our friends in the mountains all around us to give us ample warning of the approach of any enemies.

As we came up, someone threw a pile of wood on the fire so that it blazed up again. In the firelight I could make out a group of six men. They were all unshaven and unkempt, in ragged clothing, and looked a tough collection. I was too tired to do more than shake hands with each and their names meant nothing to me. They saw how tired I was and led me into the shelter where one of them showed me a pile of ragged blankets which was to be my bed. I lay down and was soon oblivious to everything.

When I woke it was still early, but my comrades were stirring.

I found myself lying between two of them, so close that we were all touching. The eight of us were tucked in tightly to our little shelter. The early morning air was chilly and there was dew on my face and hair. Outside the sun was rising and the nightingales were singing.

I was itching all over. I did not have to look very long at the blanket to discover why. The filthy rags with which I was covered were crawling with lice and fleas. They were so tattered and full of holes that it was impossible to wash them.

My companions greeted me and we took stock of each other with interest. It was Len, a sergeant in the Australian infantry, who had given me his bed the previous night. He was stretched beside me now, his long length looking longer for the trousers which only came down to his ankles. His face, like the others, was weathered to a dark brown colour and, like the others, he had a considerable growth of black stubble. It accentuated the hollowness of his cheeks. Beyond him was Les, his close companion, also a sergeant in the same battalion. Les looked like a walking scarecrow. He had had malaria even worse than the others, and it had left him like a shadow. The prolonged starvation diet had not improved matters. His skin was yellow under the tan. His eyes were bloodshot, and it was difficult to understand how he kept going at all. Only his great spirit burned bright.

On my other side was Bill, a raw-boned butcher from Sydney with fair hair and high cheekbones and a pink and white complexion. The pink and white was not very noticeable now as it was well covered by a layer of dirt and sunburn. Bill was a confirmed pessimist and looked upon the world with a gloomy eye.

Then there was Harry Brown, and his sparring partner Stuart Brown, who was no relation. Stuart was short and stocky with red hair. The Greeks called him "Kokinos" — the red. He too came from Sydney. He had a cultured, quiet manner and, with Harry, had borne much of the responsibility for the little party during their time together.

155

Beside Derek Scott lay another black-haired giant from Sydney called Mark. He looked fitter than any of the others. He had not had such bad malaria. He and Derek were an irresponsible and happy pair.

Over in the corner was a piece of human dynamite. Taffy was a Welshman and had had a colourful career. There were few things which he had not tried — for a short time at any rate. He was in his early twenties and had been in the regular army for a year or so before the war. He was one of the first volunteers to form a commando unit for specially dangerous operations. Taffy was short and broad and extremely powerful. He bounced along on his feet like a rubber ball. He was always very independent and his language was picturesque, to describe it mildly.

I was delighted to meet the Australians, most of whom belonged to the battalion in which my friend Dick Mann had served. They all knew and respected him, and I was immediately accepted as a friend of his. Derek, of course, had already given the others a highly coloured description of me. He was glad to have some Air Force support. I discovered that he and the others had made an elaborate plan to rescue me from the prison hospital. They had arranged with a local Greek to take some vegetables to the hospital in a cart. I was then to be smuggled out in the cart and driven across the country to join them here. Derek was astounded that I had managed to escape on my own and could not believe that I had come all the way on my own feet. The miracle of our meeting was quite beyond his understanding. We had to send messengers after our gallant Greek carter to warn him that I had already left.

I was touched by Derek's plan and the way everybody had combined together to work it out and make it possible. It was a constant source of amazement to find how these simple mountain folk in Greece were prepared to risk their lives time and again for us.

Breakfast was soon ready. The men had had nothing to eat for three days, so the arrival of provisions had not been untimely.

156

Our Greek guides had departed the previous night. We sat around the fire and ate slices of the wholemeal bread, toasted at the fire and then soaked in olive oil with a sprinkling of salt. It tasted very good. We drank tea made from herbs gathered off the hillside. We used to pick sage and thyme and brew them in boiling water. The resulting tea was very good. We were not particular. We took life as it came.

III

After breakfast we sat around the fire. There was nothing else to do. We talked and talked. I began to hear some of the incredible adventures which these fellows had been through.

Most of them had escaped about ten months earlier at the same time as Harry Brown. They had been travelling from Salonika to Belgrade in closed trucks, packed together tightly inside. They had filed away the locks on the doors and waited until the train was going slowly at night. Then they had hurled themselves out of the truck. One of the party had been killed under the wheels of the train. Some of them had been cut and bruised as they fell on the stones. But they were free. In pairs, they had made their way back through the mountains, heading eastwards. The Struma River was a great barrier which they had found impossible to pass. It was very closely guarded, forming the boundary between the German and the Bulgarian occupied zones.

The country on the other side of the Struma up to the Turkish border was filled with Bulgarian troops, and there were terrible tales of atrocities committed there. Whole villages were being exterminated or forced to move, and refugees were pouring westwards into Macedonia from Thrace.

My comrades had tried four or five times to get help from the monasteries at Ayon Oros, until their boots were worn out on the jagged rocks. They had been all round the coastline, looking for a friendly boat in which to hide. But their efforts had been in vain.

I was amazed at their perseverance and courage. The winter had been very hard with 30 degrees of frost and deep snow. They had been exposed to cold and weather and to the deadly malaria. Yet they had never given up. Their spirit was an inspiration.

Bill Watson had not escaped with the others. He had got away from the notorious prison-camp in Salonika. One night he had slipped out of the hut and walked quietly to the barbed wire. As when I was there, it was a double fence with about five yards of heaped barbed wire in between the two fences. At each corner of the compound stood a raised platform on which there was a searchlight and a machine-gun. The sentry would swing the searchlight from one lane of barbed wire to the other alternately throughout the night.

Bill had wrapped sacking round his legs and hands to prevent them from getting torn by the wire. He quietly cut the strands, one by one. Every time the searchlight swung over on to him he had to stand rigid, praying that he would not be seen. Slowly he worked his way across that five yards of purgatory. It took him two hours — two hours of alternating despair and hope as the searchlight swung on to and away from him. Two hours of acute fear and feverish activity. At the end of it he was through the wire but almost helpless with nervous exhaustion. Slowly he pulled himself away. There was one last obstacle to cross — a deep ditch or moat. He lowered himself down the side and was just about to drop to the bottom when a patrol came round the corner, walking along the bottom of the moat. Bill had to cling to the top of the wall with numbed fingers as the sentries approached and passed within inches of him in the darkness. After that he had got away and had met with the others later.

Stuart Brown had been nearest to success. He had actually been in a boat and they had started off to sail to Turkey. But they had not even got away from the Greek coast before a German air patrol saw them and a patrol boat was directed to inspect them. When they saw it approach they headed for the shore and beached the boat. It was a race for time and they were running up the beach as the patrol landed. Stuart got away among a hail of bullets and evaded the intensive search which followed.

Taffy's escape was one of the most picturesque. The Australian gambling game of "two-up" draws a crowd which forms up in a circle round the "ringmaster". It was a regular daily feature of prison life to see several of these rings at one time. Taffy's ring was formed around the lid of a manhole leading down to one of the old sewers of Salonika. Hidden from the sentries by the crowd, they had lifted the lid of the sewer. Every time the coins were spun a man would go forward to the middle, ostensibly to retrieve them. He would drop down the hole into the sewer. Thirteen had gone down before the Germans suspected anything. Then there was a commotion, but Taffy and the others were scuttling down the big sewer like rats and got away. No one had any idea how big the sewer was or where it led to, but they had come up all right some distance from the camp through another manhole.

At one time, Taffy had been recaptured. He passed himself off as a Greek, feigning dumbness to get over the language difficulty. The Germans were suspicious of him and put him in a Greek prison under observation. Taffy consistently refused to speak and they beat him. It was still without avail. He was transferred, from the village prison where he had been caught, to Salonika for further questioning. In the civilian prison he saw an opportunity to get away and slipped out and off to the hills again.

We spoke of the future. It seemed that our Greek friends were hopeful that they might be able to get in touch with a smuggler's boat which would secrete us on board. Arrangements were reported to have been made and the boat was to be ready in about two weeks' time. Everyone felt that I had brought good luck with me. My own adventures in reaching them were proof enough.

Derek and Mark were fretting at the delay. They craved action and only the promise of a boat in two weeks' time kept them with us. Otherwise they would have gone off on foot. The others were impatient too. They had lain up in the hills all winter. Spring had come and it was time to be moving again. I understood their feelings. My own inclination was the same. But I had the strong sense that it was right to wait. I decided that I would wait there for ever if that was the plan. I was ready to do anything that God told me. I was prepared to bet that He knew best. Once I was clear about that, my impatience vanished and I relished the time of leisure to the full.

X

IN THE MOUNTAINS

I

Life in the hills took a little getting used to. There were four main problems: how to keep warm, how to keep fed, how to keep clean and how to keep patient. Life was a constant battle with one or other of our enemies — cold and hunger, dirt and boredom. But there were compensations too. Of these the chief was the company. We got on well together; and the scenery was breath-takingly beautiful.

Dawn was usually the coldest time. We would wake shivering in the early morning chill, our bedraggled wrappings damp with the dew. Our life had a simple rhythm — we rose and lay down with the sun. Every morning I used to slip away from the others down the mountain track. A few hundred yards from our hide-out the track curled round the corner of the mountain-side and presented the most beautiful view that I had ever seen. The wooded slopes fell steeply to a narrow valley and a rushing mountain stream. On the other side, the mountains rose again, ridge after ridge, stretching away into the distance. And there, suspended in the sky like a cloud, were the massive snow-slopes of Olympus.

Southwards, the foothills dropped away to the coast and the shining Aegean, trapped between the pincers of the Khalkidiki peninsulas. To the east and north the view was limited by the precipitous slopes on which we were perched.

Every morning I used to come to this spot and sit there, drinking in the beauty of the scene as the sun rose in red or golden splendour behind the mountains. The snows on Olympus

161

would become tinged with pink or rose colour and the long shadows would draw in quickly as the sun came up. This was the time for listening to the birds. Choirs of nightingales would greet the morning in ecstatic tones.

Warmed by my brisk walk round the mountain, I would sit in this perfect setting and praise God. I used to take my little New Testament with me and read in it every morning. Then I would sit silent, seeking direction for the day and for the future. For a full hour I would sit like this, listening. Then I would walk back to join the others in the business of the day, armed with a programme, a warmth of heart, and a freedom from personal problems.

By the time I got back, breakfast, if there was any, would be ready. The fire would be burning up brightly again and we would squat round it, munching our bread and drinking the hot herb tea. Afterwards, we used to stroll down in ones and twos to the spring about a quarter of a mile away below us in order to wash.

After I had been in the hills a couple of days I discovered that I was lousy. Derek Scott and I examined every seam of every garment I was wearing, sitting naked in the sunlight as we searched. We found and killed more than two hundred lice.

Derek proceeded to boil my underpants and shirt for twenty minutes. This was guaranteed to kill off the eggs which might have escaped our search. After that, I instituted a routine search every second day and so kept the number of lice down to a minimum.

I had a sharp struggle with my conscience about cleanliness. It was not easy to strip and wash in ice-cold water on this mountain slope in spring. I resisted the conviction that it was the right thing to do. It became an issue with me as to whether I was prepared once more to do the right thing or to follow my own inclinations when these were at variance. I prayed for release from this self-interest and from then on I had no difficulty. Every day I would stand and wash myself in the ice-cold water while the brisk mountain breezes stimulated my circulation.

Every second day, instead of hunting lice, I would get Harry Brown to shave me. We could not afford the expenditure of razor blades to shave every day. But I was determined to keep up appearances, believing that they had much to do with morale. The others followed suit and we became a much more respectable-looking party.

When the business of washing was over, there was wood to be cut and collected, to keep the fire going for another twenty-four hours. My arms were useless for cutting wood so I used to go off and gather sticks for kindling. Once, as I brought back my pile of sticks to the fireside, I took one to put it on the fire and a scorpion fell off into the flames. There was consternation for a moment and thereafter we picked our firewood with more care.

About this time of day we would begin to wonder whether any visitors would arrive and, if so, what contributions would come to the kitchen. Food was never very far from our thoughts. There was usually a discussion as to whether we should ration ourselves on what we had left, on the assumption that it would have to last us for a few days more, or whether we should count on getting replenished and eat regular meals. I felt from my experience that God would provide and that He meant us to eat what the Greeks had so generously given us. So we ate what we had and were thankful. At midday we might have thick bean soup enriched with olive oil and flavoured with wild herbs. Or sometimes it would be just bread again or bread and olives. There was little variation from one meal to another, but we were not fussy.

II

In the afternoons we would lie in the sun and sleep, or stroll round the hillside. Frequently we would walk down to a lonely mountain hut which lay about a mile away from us, perched on the side of the hill — overlooking the valley and away beyond to the sea. This hut was the only human habitation in the district,

163

apart from the village three hours away. It was a little stone building with two rooms. The floor was beaten earth and the furniture home-made. Wild boarskins served as rugs and mattresses and even blankets. There was a little vegetable garden round the hut and a tiny patch of cultivation measuring perhaps two hundred yards square had been carved out of the woods.

In the hut lived a solitary old man. He was known to us all as Barba Costa. His age was indeterminate — somewhere between seventy and eighty. He was small and shrivelled with a scraggy white beard and his face was lined like old leather. But his blue eyes twinkled and his feet in their hog-skin sandals were light upon the stones. He could still out-march many a younger man.

Barba Costa was a hunter. History related that he had been married for only a short time when his young wife died. At that time they had been living in the village and young Costa sweated his living off the land. The tragedy of his young wife's death broke his heart and he retired to the mountains. Nobody saw him for a long time. He built himself this little house with his own hands and settled down in it. With incredible energy, he had cleared little patches of ground here and there on the mountains, ploughing them by hand himself and sowing his own wheat. He became practically self-supporting, growing his own food, making his own clothes, looking after himself.

A further tragedy occurred when his brother was shot as a bandit in some skirmish. It is not unlikely that Barba Costa himself indulged in a little banditry from time to time in his young days. Later he had lived up there in the mountains as a hunter. He hunted wild boar and got to know them so well that he looked like one himself with his white bristles and his small twinkling eyes. He could move through the woods without a sound and he knew every trail and every stick and stone for miles around. He would trap and shoot the wild boar and any other game that was about. There were occasional hares and partridges; and even some wolves and bears. Barba Costa knew them all.

164

Once, in some distant adventure, he had fallen heavily and broken his right shoulder. Not being able to avail himself of any medical assistance, his shoulder had healed up in rather a mess and it was anchylosed like my own. This was a great link between us and the old man would come over to me and pat my shoulder gently and smile and lift his own crippled arm to show its limited movement. He was devoted to us all; our adventures were after his own heart and like him we loved the mountains. Bill used to go down to see him most days to help him to cultivate his fields. Barba Costa was invariably cheerful. He had a great sense of humour with philosophy too, and Bill's gloom was perceptibly lightened after his visits to the old man.

Sometimes of an afternoon, Barba Costa would come up to visit us in our hide-out. He would appear suddenly, coming out from the trees like a merry little wraith with his toothless grin and high-pitched laugh. His clothes were a constant source of amusement. He would appear wrapped up in the most extraordinary collection of wild animal skins. Then he would sit down by the fire and tell us stories or listen to our tales of home. Harry and Stuart Brown spoke quite good Greek and most of the others had a smattering with which they could carry on a conversation. Stuart Brown was a special favourite with the old man.

One day, while the old man was with us, we heard a familiar call — "Yasou" — from down the hillside. It was some of our friends from the village coming up to see us. As usual they brought a sack of provisions with them. With them was a stranger. He was well dressed by comparison with our village friends. He wore a dark blue suit and looked incongruous on the hillside. He was a young man and it appeared that he had come all the way from Salonika, five days' march, to see us. I never discovered whose friend he was in particular, but in some mysterious way he had been included in Derek Scott's fantastic plans for rescuing me. He had come to meet us and to take our picture. He had an ancient box Brownie camera with him and one photograph left on the spool. We made up a group for him to photograph. Barba Costa was delighted to be included with us. Our friend made a note of our home addresses and promised to send us copies after the war. I was sent the historic picture two years later in London.

Another day some ladies visited us. We heard they were coming and made great preparations to receive them. We had a special brew of herb tea ready and our camp was especially tidy and clean. It was our friend Agapitos who had entertained me on my first evening in Ormelia, with his wife, and they brought with them a middle-aged widow who owned a mill nearby. She had had to evacuate from Thrace when the Bulgarians came in. Her mill and home were burned down and she fled to these friends in Macedonia. Here she had established another mill and was doing as brisk a trade as the times permitted. It was she, apparently, who had given much of the bread on which we subsisted.

Our guests were regaled with vivid stories of adventure as one or other of our party would describe his escape. They stayed for just the correct time as if they were visiting the house of some friends for afternoon tea. Before they left, we showed them round and they dutifully admired our kitchen arrangements and our quarters, specially tidied for the occasion. As they left, the good ladies volunteered to do all our mending for us. We could not help laughing at this point. They looked at our bedraggled figures, clad in rags, and joined in the general laughter. Nevertheless they took away a coat of Stuart's to be mended, and my jacket to be dyed a less conspicuous colour.

Their visit was timely in many ways. We had completely run out of food and the miller's wife had brought some cream cheese for us, a great delicacy. But the biggest surprise of all was to find a good sized joint of mutton in the bag. It was the first meat we had seen for a long time. We had a royal feast and the bones made delicious soup for several days. Finally, softened by much boiling, we ate them too.

166

As the day wore on, we would gradually congregate round the camp fire. I usually took a last stroll round to my vantage-point on the hillside where I would watch the sun sink in blazing splendour behind Olympus. The flaming sky silhouetted the darkening peaks as the shadows grew more and more intense. The colours fading left a warm glow as the distant scene grew dim. As I walked back, the nightingales would be singing, and the camp fire was a bright beacon through the trees.

The evening air grew quickly cold, but we were cosy by the leaping flames of our fire. We would squat there, talking of trifles or silent for long intervals. The firelight glowed ruddily on bronzed faces. Our herb tea would be brewing and we would sit there, sipping it. Soon it would be time to go to bed.

Together we would move towards our sleeping quarters, piling fresh branches on the fire to keep it going all night. The blaze was our light for going to bed.

It was quite a problem getting into bed; the blankets were so frail and had to be adjusted with meticulous care to leave no holes. We slept fully dressed, simply taking our footwear off. We were packed tightly together, side by side. I seldom had difficulty in going to sleep. But in the first few days up there I found the rats rather a trial.

They were clean country rats and much smaller than the big sewer rats which we had at Salonika. But they were extremely bold. As soon as all was quiet, they would start scurrying about inside the shelter. There would be little squeaks and scuttling among the leaves. Then one would run across the row of sleeping bodies. Another would follow and you could feel their feet patter on the coverings. They even ran across your head. That was too much for me and I used to sleep with my woollen bala-clava helmet on and a scarf across my face. After that I was not disturbed, even when they ran across my face.

The others used to set traps for them. Bill was a handyman at this sort of thing. He had discovered how to make a simple form of trap from some of the shepherds. It consisted of a large flat stone which was supported at an angle of about forty-five degrees by a piece of stick. A system of simple levers and carefully adjusted balances ended in a piece of pointed stick on which we would put a morsel of bread. The rats would come in and nibble at the bread; this upset the balance and the stone would fall, killing them instantly. We had great success with our trap, sometimes killing two or three rats before going to sleep.

We had one spell of bad weather and it gave me an insight into what conditions must have been like for the others during the winter. The mists swirled by, and the snow piled up for a brief hour before it melted away to join the torrents which rushed down the hillside. It was bitterly cold; our shelter was little protection from the wind, and water poured through several places in the roof. We all got soaked with our bedding too. It was rough for a few days and we were never really dry or warm. But then the weather cleared again and we put all our bedding out on the hillside in the sun and picked fresh heather for our mattresses.

The rain too had its compensations. It brought out a wonderful crop of snails. We hastened to collect them. They were big, juicy snails, carrying their big round shells laboriously over the wet grass. The Greek custom was to take a long thin stick with pointed end and a T-piece at the bottom and spear the snail through its shell. If you put them in a bag they quickly crawled out. We cooked them in two different ways. The civilised way was to boil them in salt water. They were inclined to be tasteless prepared this way without the sauces and subtleties of a French chef. The other way was to roast them in the ashes of the fire. You simply put the shell in the hot ashes and waited until it looked right. Snail done this way was very tasty as well as nourishing.

The shepherds taught us this. We were visited by them frequently. They were generally young boys, occasionally very young. One trio in charge of nearly two hundred goats came from a village which was a day's march away across the hills.

There was a small boy of about eight years old, clad like his elder brothers in goatskins. The others were about twelve and sixteen years old respectively. The youngest came bounding across the crags, as sure-footed as one of his own goats. It was strange to see these lads, prematurely grown up with adult responsibilities.

Their job was to lead the herd of goats across the hills, feeding as they went, off the young leaves and occasional patches of grass. The goats were huge creatures, as wild and wary as deer. But the lads had an amazing knowledge of them, they knew each goat individually by name. They would catch two or three and milk them for us. The small boy would hurl himself across twenty yards of open clearing to fall triumphantly on the heels of a goat in a flying tackle. Some of us tried to catch them too, and were completely unsuccessful. The boys laughed at our ineptitude.

The goats' milk was a very welcome addition to our diet and we valued our shepherd visitors for more than their company. But they were an entertaining trio too. We would sit in the gloaming round the fire while the eldest boy played on his pipes. The pipes were hollow tubes of wood, carved by the shepherds. Their thin soft notes haunted the memory, carrying one back across the centuries. Here, in the ancient home of freedom, time was just another toy to be taken up or laid down at will.

The boys led their goats through the mountains for weeks on end. Usually two of them would be with the herd while the third was visiting the village, collecting their bread. He would be away for about three days and when he came back another would go. At nights they slept out with the herd. Just before dark they would start to build a thorn enclosure. They were very quick at this, cutting the wood and driving it into the ground with the certainty of long practice. Very soon the enclosure would be complete, standing about six or seven feet high — strong enough to keep the goats in and the wolves out.

Just outside the enclosure the boys would build themselves a little lean-to hut out of brushwood. Beside it would be a huge pile of firewood to replenish the bonfire, which they would keep blazing throughout the night. The fire served the double purpose of keeping them warm and keeping the wolves away.

As a further protection against the wolves and any other marauders, they had their pack of dogs, huge white animals which would attack anything that approached. We would go down sometimes to visit them after dark. The dogs would come bounding out to attack us, but a call from one of the boys would be enough to send them padding back to the enclosure.

The boys were very partial to a cigarette and while they heated up a big pot of goats' milk for us my Australian friends would roll cigarettes with deft fingers. Then we would sit around the blazing fire, drinking the hot milk and listening to the weird haunting music of the pipes.

IV

There were times when we would see nobody for several days. Frequently we went for two days without food. This did not trouble us much. We were well accustomed by now to irregular meals. On one occasion, however, four days went by without our having anything to eat. For men in good condition this would not have been bad, but for us, who had been living near starvation for many months, it was serious. It was a common experience, even when we were feeding regularly, to have black-outs when we stood up quickly, but at the end of this period we began to show further signs of wear. We became weak and indifferent.

The others began to get very concerned about the food situation. But every morning, during my meditations on the mountainside, I had the promise that God would provide everything necessary. I was given a freedom from concern which surprised me no less than the others.

Whenever the question of food occurred in the conversation, as it frequently did, I would remind the others how, on previous occasions when we had feared the worst, my hunch had always worked out. We called it "Howell's luck" and it became the one factor which kept us together. Without our belief in it, we should have split up long before and gone our separate ways about the countryside where the chances of picking up food appeared more certain.

Towards the end of the fourth day, we agreed that somebody would have to go down to the village to explain our plight if no food arrived. But I felt that this would not be necessary and I was right. Just before dusk, two figures appeared, staggering under a huge sack of supplies. We welcomed them with more than usual warmth. The man carrying the sack was a Cypriot soldier called Georgios Petrou.

George was a big, strapping fellow of about forty who came from Limassol in Cyprus. He had been serving with a Cypriot labour battalion in Greece and had been cut off by the Germans from being evacuated. George had taken to the hills where his Greek ancestry and native Greek language stood him in good stead. He could not be distinguished from the local inhabitants and it was easy for him to move about the country as a Greek.

From my companions, I learned that George had been one of their most faithful and courageous supporters during the hard days in the winter. He had walked many miles to collect and bring food to them. I liked the look of him and we chatted together about Cyprus, which I had visited a couple of years before on leave. George was very pessimistic about our chances of getting away from Greece. He himself, in spite of his ability to disguise himself as a Greek, had found it impossible to get across to Turkey. No boat captain would take the chance of being caught smuggling someone out, and the journey across Thrace on foot was out of the question because of the large numbers of Bulgarian troops in every village.

We had learned much together during these four days of fasting. It had been a battle to remain united. Hungry people quarrel even more readily than when they are well fed. And the strong tendency to split up and go roving again was accentuated

171

by the need for food. But we had won through and our victory established even closer links between us. I was more than ever confident that God had a plan for us for the future and further miracles would result. So I told George that it would not be long before he would be back home in Cyprus. He was evidently impressed by my confidence and sincerity and his gloom was perceptibly lightened.

His companion had been greeted by loud cheers from the others. Evidently he was an old friend. He was introduced to me as Anastasios and his nickname was "The Little Father of all the English". He was a small man with twinkling eyes and he wore the light-grey uniform of the Greek country police or agrofilax. His job was to oversee the country districts and enforce law and order. His self-appointed role was to look after us.

During the winter, Anastasios had walked hundreds of miles through the snow collecting provisions from outlying districts to keep my friends alive. He was untiring in his efforts and regardless of his own health and safety. Worn out with his exertions he had had a heart attack some weeks ago and had nearly died. This was his first visit for some time and he still had to go slowly. I thanked him for all his care of my friends.

We sat down together round the fire and broke bread. We did not trouble to toast it or to cook anything. We just ate. After a long period of hunger, a little food goes a long way. You eat little and often. The digestion cannot deal with a huge quantity of food at one time. It has to be developed again, little by little. So we did not eat much; but what we ate tasted very good. It was dark when George and Anastasios left to go. They had a four-hour march in front of them. George was sharing house with Anastasios in a nearby village. They promised to come and see us again soon.

We sat on, far into the night, talking. We ate again before going to bed. My friends were very interested in the way things had worked out. We spoke of the future and the need for a new spirit to be kindled everywhere if the sacrifice of war was to be worth while. We spoke of the fundamental causes of war, the fears, hatreds and greeds lying deep down in the hearts of people. These were the things with which we must grapple if we were to build a new world.

My tough friend, Taffy, sat silent as I proclaimed my belief that God really could change the hearts and way of living of men and nations. This was the simple belief that most of us had been brought up with, but had somehow lost in the rush and scramble of everyday living. It was a forgotten factor for most of us, until we got into such trouble that we turned back to our childhood to try it as a last desperate resort.

Taffy had not had the benefits or background that most of us had been born with. This talk of God was news to him. It was something he did not understand. For once, he was a silent and interested listener. The following morning, when I came back from the hillside, he asked me to lend him my New Testament. He sat throughout the morning, poring over it with fresh interest, and his language was a little modified for a time. I had further talks with some of the others. Whatever else may have resulted from our time together, we were certainly given a new comradeship and closeness.

V

After we had been in the hills about two weeks, we had word through George Petrou that the plans for the boat were delayed for a week. This announcement brought a crisis in the camp. Derek and Mark were fretting to get on the road. The others were of a similar mind. But my strong feeling was that we should stick together. I had no guarantee what would happen or where we should go, but I did feel that whatever happened we were meant to be together.

I put it to the others that "Howell's luck" had never let them down. I was sure that it would not let them down now. This was no idle remark. I was convinced in my own mind and the others knew it. My conviction was the deciding factor. They agreed to stay with me for another week.

At the end of this time, George appeared again, this time with the news that the project had failed. The boat which they had hoped to obtain would sail without us. The captain and crew were finally unwilling to take the risk, although they had been offered a very large sum of money by our friends.

This was too much for the rebels. Derek and Mark could be restrained no longer. They decided to go. Derek was apologetic to me but he was clearly impatient with what he thought was my lack of enterprise. No persuasion had any avail with him. So I gave him a new pair of woollen socks which I had in reserve and together we saw that he and Mark were as properly equipped for the road as possible. We walked round the corner of the hill in the sunshine with them and stood watching their figures dwindle into the distance. A pair of golden eagles swung round the cliffs. They floated on effortless wings and their golden plumage was bright against the blue of the sky. They were hunting and came so close that I could see every detail of their cruel claws and great curved beaks. There was something symbolic about the scene, for the shadow of the Nazi Eagle was already dark upon my friends. They were recaptured not long after and spent the rest of the war in Germany.

The others were restive too. Les and Len were keen to take to the road together again. We agreed to let Derek and Mark have a good start so that there would be no crossing of trails or competition for food and shelter. Les and Len decided to pay a visit to the nearby village where Anastasios lived, to thank the village folk for all their support during these long months. If anything developed in the meantime we could send a message down to Ormelia, where they would call before going on into the unknown. The next day they too went off.

Typically, Taffy wanted to go off on his own. He would not be restrained. So he left the same day as Les and Len in another direction. I watched them go with regret, but there was nothing I could do to persuade them that we should stick together. They had lost faith when the boat on which they had been relying had not materialised.

I had a struggle myself to avoid losing faith at this point. I too had somehow taken it for granted that the plan would work out in that particular way. But I was soon reassured in my mind. God had not brought us together like this for nothing. The others believed me. Stuart and Harry said that they would stay on and strangely enough Bill, the pessimist, also elected to stay with me. I was grateful for them. To relieve the boredom, Stuart and Harry decided to go on down to Anastasios' village for a few days to see their friends down there. Then they too would head for Ormelia and see if there was any news.

This left me alone in the hills with Bill. Of all the members of our party, he was the one I least wanted to be left alone with. I thought him an unsociable and gloomy companion. But my attitude changed; I recognised how good he had been with Barba Costa, helping him in the fields; and I remembered that he, more than any of the others, had won the hearts of our shepherd friends. So Bill and I became friends and got to know each other well during these last days together. While we were there alone the shepherds arrived and we fed luxuriously on bread and milk.

Then one morning my original guides from Ormelia, Mitsios and Alekko, appeared again. They had visited us several times with gifts of food, but this time they had come for another reason. Mitsios' face was beaming, and old Barba Costa came with them from his hut with his toothless grin, his old gun slung over his shoulder.

They were mysterious about details, but said that there were prospects of getting two of us away at any rate. They felt that I should go first, to see if I could arrange with the British authorities to rescue the others. We were to go immediately and stay until further notice at the little villa by the sea where I had been before.

Now that the time had come to go, I was sad to leave our home in the mountains. I looked on while Mitsios and Alekko and Bill tore down our shelter and scattered it about the hillside, to leave as little trace as possible. Our tattered blankets and our few utensils were to go to Barba Costa for the meantime.

Above all, I was sad to say good-bye to the old man. We had grown to love him dearly, and Bill and I had become his special friends. But he was philosophic as ever. He had seen friends come and go. We should meet again somewhere — sometime. His faith was simple and his philosophy sound. He had weathered the storms of more than three score years alone. He was serene and untroubled.

We walked down to his little hut together, Bill on one side of him and I on the other. We said little, but our companionship was none the less close. He had been through so many of our own experiences that we knew each other perfectly. Barba Costa had starved when we had starved. He had eaten when we had eaten, and been cold when we were cold. But this was nothing new to him. It was part of a lifelong struggle which he had fought and won.

He symbolised for me the eternal fighting spirit of Greece. Undaunted by hardship and misfortune, his spirit moved as freely as the winds that blew among his beloved mountains. He might be poor and cold and hungry and old, but Barba Costa was free; he too had escaped to live.

Mitsios and Alekko deposited their burden of blankets and utensils in his little hut. Bill hoisted his own belongings on his broad back and we said good-bye to the old man. He stood there, a solitary figure on the hillside, his white beard waving in the breeze, until we were out of sight.

XI

AYON OROS — SACRED MOUNTAIN

I

We walked slowly down the mountainside. Mitsios explained that for safety we should not enter the village before dusk. The track led us down the wooded slopes into the valley. We crossed great gorges, already lying in shadow, with mountain streams plunging down them. It was my first sight of this country, as it had been dark when I came up three weeks before.

The warm afternoon air held the scent of sage and pine-trees. Down in the valley we wandered through pleasant groves and little meadows. We stopped frequently for rests; we were in no hurry. Alekko pointed out the site of a Roman encampment. The moat and buttresses were still there, outlined in the turf. Everywhere, in this part of Greece, the valleys were rich in history; farmers were constantly turning up precious pieces of pottery, coins and sculptures.

Towards dusk we came to the river again which I had had difficulty in crossing on my arrival. This time we came to it at a place where it ran broad and shallow over a gravel bed. I was about to take off my boots in order to wade across with the others, when Mitsios picked me up and carried me over on his back.

Strolling on through the growing shadows, we passed a little white church, standing by itself on a mound. Easter had been celebrated here only a few days before with flowers and festival. The feast of freedom was an omen, both for ourselves and ultimately for the nation.

Coming into the outskirts of the village we were silent and

177

walked in single file, keeping to the shadows. Alekko led us straight into his house. Inside, we found another gathering of our friends. Anastasios was there, our "Little Father". The children clustered round us and Alekko's wife busied herself with some other wives around the open fire.

Soon we were seated round the room on the floor with a little low table set in front of us. It was a farewell feast. Our friends had gone round, collecting food for this special occasion. There was fish, deliciously cooked, and fresh bread and peta. We were overwhelmed with the kindness of these simple folk who were risking their lives to give us this final outstanding evidence of their care.

Soon it was time to go and we said our last farewells to everybody. I was overcome with emotion and could not express my gratitude, but I think that they understood. Silently we slipped out into the night where a cart was waiting. Bill and I clambered into the back and were covered up with sacks. Then we drove off along the bumpy trail towards the sea.

Clear of the village, we sat up on the edge of the cart. Mitsios and Alekko and Anastasios were our companions and guides. The moon was up and cast its soft light on the quiet countryside. We met no one as we jogged along at an easy walking pace. We were bound for the little white villa by the sea.

I discovered that it belonged to the brother of Agapitos. His name was Angelos Agapitos and he was a rich businessman from Salonika. We had not met him, but it had been he who had previously negotiated for a boat for us.

We stopped the cart well short of the villa and Mitsios and Anastasios went ahead to prospect. Everything was all right and Angelos Agapitos was there together with his caretaker, the old man who had previously looked after me. They were expecting us. Angelos greeted us warmly. He was of middle age and medium height, generously built. He spoke French, not fluently but about my own standard. We understood each other easily.

He explained that he had a friend who was trying to lead a

party of twenty Greek officers out of the country to join their army in Egypt. They had hired a smuggler's boat for a million drachma, a fabulous sum, collected from all their friends and relatives, and they were trying to persuade the captain of the boat to agree to take me with them. The boat was small and there would only be room for one person. They all felt that I was the one to go since I could use my influence to try to arrange for the others to be rescued by a submarine or some other means.

Bill was not really disappointed. He had expected this, in his usual gloomy way. He was generous and unselfish about it. I felt that it was right for me to go if it worked out as we hoped. In the meantime, Bill and I were to wait in the villa of Agapitos until we heard if the captain had agreed to take me and, if so, when we should leave.

In some way which I could not fully understand, the people into whose farm I had been so miraculously led were involved in this too. Their nephew, whom I had not met there, was to be one of the party. The threads of my previous adventures were being woven together into a pattern.

Mitsios and Anastasios said good-bye. It was impossible to thank them for all that they had done. We spoke of our next meeting, hopefully, hanging on to the last traces of our happy relationship. I gave them messages for Stuart and Harry and the others, telling them to remain in the district and in touch with Agapitos. I promised to make arrangements for their escape.

Bill and I slept soundly in the little white villa on the hill. The wind sighed through the pines and the waves chattered on the beach below.

In the morning, Angelos and Bill and I sat in the shadow of an olive tree. One of Angelos's concerns was the manufacture of olive oil and he owned an oil factory and many orchards. He described the process by which the olives are ripened, gathered and pressed to yield their precious oil.

At noon, we sat round a little table under the trees and ate a delicious lunch of fresh fish and bread and olives. The fish had been caught that morning in the bay just off the beach. One had firm, pink flesh and was very tasty. There was also some squid, and Bill and I ate with relish.

After lunch, Agapitos left us. The plans were laid and his part was accomplished for the meantime. I promised to keep in touch with him about the others and thanked him for all he was doing for us. Then Bill and I lay in the shade throughout the long, drowsy afternoon and dozed.

Early in the evening a visitor arrived. He was a young man with an engaging smile. He was one of the young officers from the escaping party. But he brought bad news. The captain was unwilling to take me. I was bitterly disappointed.

Our envoy's name was Agamemnon Panagatopoulos. He explained in good French that his friends called him Memni. It was easier. He was hopeful that the captain would change his mind and said that negotiations were still proceeding to that end. In the meantime, he had to return to the others. They would call at the villa on the following evening after dark on their way to the boat. I should not know until then whether they were able to take me or not, but I had to be ready to leave.

He went off again and Bill and I were left alone. I realised how much I had been building my hopes on the prospect of escape this time. I prayed that I might seek and accept what God had in store for me, whatever it might be, even if it meant my staying indefinitely where I was. With that my inward peace returned, and I was no longer troubled with doubts and fears about the future. Bill and I sat chatting happily together.

The next day passed peacefully at the villa. We lazed about the hillside. The old caretaker cooked our meals for us, so we lived in luxury by comparison with our time in the hills. As evening drew on I had twinges of self-concern about whether or not I should go. But now I knew the secret and I remained largely free. The dusk deepened into darkness and still there was no sign of anyone. We ate our evening meal quietly, listening for a knock at the door.

We had almost decided that nobody would come when the long-awaited knock at the door came. Bill and I remained hidden in the inner room while the old man opened the door to inspect the visitors. It was all right. The party had arrived. They streamed into the little hall of the villa, twenty Greek officers of various ranks and ages. Memni came forward and introduced me to the leader of the party, Major Constas. The major was a dynamic little man. Short and broad, he moved and spoke quickly and decisively. His black eyes sparkled and he emanated confidence and capability.

I hesitated to broach the question of my departure. I was introduced all round. Then it came out. They could take me. The captain had eventually agreed.

"Can you walk to Nikiti?" the major asked me.

"I can walk a thousand miles to freedom," I replied.

They laughed and Bill helped me lace my boots and put on my coat. We said good-bye at the doorway, under the stars. I was sad to leave him for we had become firm friends during these days we had together. I left him the pocket compass which Macnamara had given me back in the hospital. He promised to wait in touch with Agapitos until he should hear from me or until he himself was able to get away. He also carried messages for the others. We pledged to meet one day in Sydney and parted.

II

We moved off in the darkness down the hill and on to the little road which skirted the beach. There we split into threes and fours and walked off briskly eastwards. I went with Major Constas and Memni. We spoke occasionally in subdued tones, though it was late at night and there was no one about. On the whole we were silent, conserving our strength.

The major walked in the same determined manner that he spoke. He radiated energy and enthusiasm. Memni was a delightful companion. He was a chemical engineer in peace-

181

time, and had joined the army on the outbreak of war, fighting with the infantry in Albania. Later, during the retreat, he had been on the staff. He constituted himself my assistant and aide. We came to the mouth of a river and waded across, bare-legged.

On through the night we marched. The pace was too fast for me and I became very weary, hardly noticing where we were, or anything except the problem of putting one foot in front of the other fast enough to keep up with the major. We stopped at a village, empty in the dark night hours, and refreshed ourselves at a spring with draughts of ice-cold water.

Then we were off again. I was unconscious of time or distance. The march became a matter of concentrating on the next stretch immediately ahead to keep up with the others. When we reached Nikiti I was blind and deaf and dumb with fatigue. When the party stopped I fell by the side of the road — blissful that I had to walk no further.

I had no recollection of how long I lay there; it was still dark when they roused me to say that we were off again. This time we were to travel by boat. There were two rowing-boats by the side of a long jetty. We clambered aboard and I immediately settled down to sleep again.

I remembered little of the next stage of the journey. Once or twice I woke to see the stars swaying overhead and hear the creak and splash of the oars.

At daybreak we were close in to a rocky shore with the hills rising steeply from the water. There was no sign of human habitation anywhere. We were moving down the long finger of the Sithonia peninsula. I slept again.

Eventually we reached our goal. The peninsula has a tiny island called Yerochristos near its tip. It is separated from the mainland by a narrow neck of shingle and it is possible to walk across unless there is a high wind blowing, when the waves make it impassable. This was where we were to hide. Our boat was to pick us up here.

We disembarked on the shingly beach and walked straight

182

up into the brushwood. The rowing-boats departed for the long journey back to Nikiti. Memni and I selected a good, thick clump of bushes and lay down inside them.

The rest of the day passed peacefully enough. There was a brief commotion when it was reported that a German patrol was about to pass close by our hiding-place; but it was a false alarm. It was only two harmless fishermen and they did not see us.

At nightfall we moved out of our hiding-places and filtered in twos and threes towards a solitary house on the island. We congregated inside and were greeted by the owner, Mr. Yerochristos, who was in some way related to Agapitos. Everybody seemed to be a relation of everybody else in this part of the world.

Twenty-one officers crowded into the little room, lit by a flickering oil-lamp. The provisions were produced, bread and olives. We ate gratefully. Afterwards, we settled down to sleep wherever we were. People were stretched on the floor in every corner of the room. Memni procured a couch for me and one for the major and slept beneath us on the floor.

The following day we went back to our hiding-place in the bushes during the daylight hours. I was much refreshed by the rest and began to have qualms of impatience. I discovered that the others had expected the boat to pick us up the day before and there was general uneasiness in case something might have happened to it.

I went off by myself to collect my thoughts and to get my mind clear again, and was once more relieved of all impatience and worry. I was prepared for anything. My mind was even reconciled to the prospect of walking all the way back to Nikiti and beyond, if that was the plan. But my hunch was that the present task was to wait and see and to make the most of my time making friends with my Greek comrades.

I went back to find Memni. His cheerfulness was somewhat damped by the delay. But soon we were laughing together and we collected some others round us. Talking took away the tension.

In the afternoon it was very hot and we were perspiring and sticky. I longed to plunge into the cool clear water. I asked the major if he would mind if we went for a swim. He seemed surprised that anyone should want to bathe if they did not have to, but he agreed that it would be quite safe for one or two of us to go down at a time, provided there was no one else in sight. So Memni and I went off to the beach, stripped and plunged into the sea.

The water was cold and invigorating. It was my first attempt to swim since I had been wounded and I found that my arms were very little use to me. I had to swim on my back so that no arm action was required. There was a little sandy strip on the beach and Memni and I ran up and down it until we were dry. Then we dressed again and joined the others.

Just before dusk we sighted a small boat sailing towards us from the west. As it drew closer, speculation mounted. It was not until it beached that we were certain it was our boat. The major went down to talk to the captain while we remained in hiding. He came back announcing that we would go aboard after dark.

After two days' waiting, the others were very excited. I was surprised at my own calmness. I was pleased but not elated. I hoped that I had learned my lesson not to presume too much upon the future.

After dark we went down to the beach and boarded the boat. It was a small caique or fishing-boat about twenty feet long. Decked in, it had a small diesel engine in addition to the sail. The captain was villainous-looking with a scraggy beard and a squint. He was voluble and gesticulated violently. He had two assistants who looked equally villainous. There was much argument between them and my comrades in voluble Greek. I had no idea what it was all about.

Eventually, all twenty-one of us had to crowd in under the decks in the hold of the ship. Now I understood why they had said there was only room for one. I began to think that they had overestimated. We were squashed in on top of one another

184

so tightly that it would have been difficult to accommodate a cat.

We cast off and the motor started up, making a chugging noise and emitting poisonous fumes of diesel oil. We were running before the wind with the sail up and the engine going as well. The hours passed uneasily. I learned that we were heading at last for Ayon Oros. We were to visit the sacred mountain after all.

III

It was pitch black there in the hold of the little boat. We were running fast before the wind. Fortunately the sea was not very rough and the Greeks were all good sailors. There was no room for anyone to be sick. We hardly considered the threat of interception by a German sea patrol. We were so cramped that we were kept preoccupied with our discomfort. I sat with my back against the ribs of the boat and my knees touching my chin. In front and on either side I was tightly pressed by my companions. There was no room to move and scarcely enough to breathe.

As time passed, one became oblivious even to the noise and smell of the engine and the splash of water on the sides of the boat. Each minute seemed the last one could endure in that position. I gathered from the others that the captain would not hear of any of us being above decks in case we should suddenly be illuminated in the patrol's searchlight. As it was strictly forbidden for any boat to operate in the Aegean by day or night without German permission, it did not seem to me to matter much whether we were seen or not. If the boat was intercepted it would be fired on — so we might as well be comfortable.

However, this did not meet with approval. The captain would refuse to take us any further unless we obeyed his orders implicitly. So we had to endure in silence. At last we heard the engine switched off. We were close in to land. This was Ayon Oros, the sacred mountain, the gateway to freedom.

Not until we beached were we allowed to come up on deck. It was difficult to move after having been in one position for so long, but it was an exquisite relief to be able to stretch once more. We breathed the cool night air with relish.

We found ourselves lying in a little cove called Kapsokalyvia. The cliffs towered two hundred feet above the surf, and beyond the mountains rose steep against the stars. Our little boat was pitching as the breakers rose and fell. The surf stretched white from our bows up on to the steep shingle. We had to get ashore from the deck down a narrow plank held at one end by a sailor. The others were having difficulty in balancing as they ran down it. I was the last to go. I debated whether to jump off the bows into the shallow water and then wade in, or try to reach shore dry footed down the plank. Something in me told me to jump off the bow, but my pride rebelled. If the others could walk ashore, so could I. I stepped on to the heaving gangway.

Without the use of my arms for balance, it was very difficult. The plank was wet and slippery and my injured hands could not grip a nearby rope. I got about halfway down and then started to lose my balance. I tried to run the remainder of the way but my feet slipped and I fell headlong into the surf, uanble to break my fall with my useless arms. As I disappeared, however, Memni rushed into the water and pulled me out, unhurt but dripping wet from head to foot. Pride had certainly come before a fall.

I stood shivering on the beach while the major outlined the plan. The boat would sail round to another cove nearby. We were all to hide during the day and re-embark at dusk for our final bid for freedom. We were to cross the Aegean to the Turkish island of Imbros to arrive there early the next morning. By so doing we hoped to evade the German air patrol which covered the water between the mainland and the islands just before eight o'clock every morning. If this aircraft spotted any boats they were attacked and sunk. So we had to be there before eight and we should only go if wind and sea were favourable. We should have to take a chance with any sea patrols.

There was not room for all of us to hide on our little beach. We should have to scale the cliffs and climb up the mountain-side to find adequate cover. The party moved off and started to climb. All were experts, since every Greek fighting man is a mountaineer. I felt that rock climbing without the use of my arms was unnecessarily hazardous and the major agreed that I should stay on the beach. I could keep out of sight behind some rocks throughout the day.

The others went on, but Memni stayed with me despite my protests. He insisted that I should take off my clothes as I was still shivering in the chill breeze of the early morning. I did what I was told and stripped. It was bitterly cold. Memni took off his own own coat and trousers and socks and insisted on my wearing them while he sat in his shirt and underclothes. I accepted gratefully, and we crouched together behind a rock out of the wind and waited for the dawn.

IV

The sun came up and my clothes quickly dried. We sat warming ourselves until it became too hot; then we moved into the shade. The day passed peacefully. All that we could see were the towering cliffs and the sparkling Aegean stretching away into the distance. Somewhere, out there, was freedom. We sat and contemplated it.

I was curious about Ayon Oros. At one time, I had even thought of retiring to a monastery here, like so many others had done across the centuries. Cut off from the world, and separated from some temptations at least, surely one could find release from worldly cares. But was that an end in itself? I could not feel that it was. If Peter and Paul and the others had retired from the world, the history of civilisation would have been very different.

For me, Ayon Oros was a gateway — the gateway to freedom. Somehow the intricate web of life had to pass through it and out into the unknown. The sacred mountain was symbolic.

Some would linger in the gateway on the brink of discovery, hesitating to launch out into the unknown, fearful of the steps to freedom though eager to attain to it. They would see in the lonely places of Ayon Oros the pale reflection of their goal. Others, however, would come to this place in their spirits and, seeing the road ahead, would step out boldly to savour the full adventure of freedom itself. These men would pioneer the trail again and shape the future.

Memni and I sat in the shade as the hours went by. We became very thirsty and found a little stream close at hand to which we made frequent expeditions to drink. We chatted idly or sat silent — absorbed in thought. I had no sense of apprehension about the future, I was simply curious to see what would happen. There was no more that I could do except sit patiently and wait.

At dusk the others appeared again, climbing down the cliff. They were extremely thirsty as there had been no water up on the hillside where they had been hiding. They made a rush for our spring.

The boat appeared and beached. The captain had also been up the hill during the day but he had certainly not been thirsty. He had visited a nearby monastery and had clearly found congenial company there. Evidently temperance was a plant which did not grow in every corner of Ayon Oros. It would certainly take more than a sacred mountain to make our captain sober.

However, his nerve was apparently fortified for the long crossing, although he still insisted on us going below deck again. We stowed ourselves obediently below and the motor chugged away once more. The discomfort of our position, the fumes, and the splash of the water again occupied our minds as we ploughed our way through a gentle swell eastwards on the last lap to liberty. It was now or never.

I sat quiet and prayed for release from every kind of self-concern. My backache ceased to trouble me and I had no worries about the future. We should escape or not — the matter was out of my hands.

After some hours the motor required replenishment with oil. A sailor stood swaying over it trying to pour oil from a drum into the tank. Oil was spilling everywhere. Suddenly it went on fire.

The scene was indescribable. Flames leapt high into the air, lighting up the surrounding sea and turning the boat into a beacon which no patrol within sight could miss. Some of our party were wedged tightly against the bulkhead by the engine. Scorched by the fire they tried in vain to compress the human cargo; they could not get away. Fortunately, the fire never became hot enough to do them serious damage, but we were not to know that. The excitement was intense. The crew were shouting and gesticulating on deck and my friends were shouting and trying to gesticulate below. Owing to the lack of space gesticulation was difficult if not dangerous.

In between dodging my neighbour's elbow, I watched the scene and could not help laughing. Memni saw the humour of the situation too, and we roared with laughter. Our immediate neighbours became slightly less energetic. I started to sing — a faovurite song of the Greek Army which I had learnt in the hills. The others gradually joined in and the din became considerably more tuneful. By this time, the crew had found a blanket and the flames were eventually smothered. We sat quiet again. Up on deck our villainous captain was humming under his boozy breath. Everyone was happy.

Somehow we had managed to escape notice and we moved steadily through the night towards our goal. It must have been about four o'clock in the morning when the captain announced that we were approaching the island. The news was greeted with tremendous enthusiasm. There was more gesticulating. We sang and cheered. We thought we were free.

We beached in another little cove and this time I jumped ashore. We thanked our alcoholic captain who was already obviously contemplating a nap. Then we set off cheerfully up the cliffs and on to the hillside. It was still very dark. Memni and I walked together. The others were noisily enthusiastic, but I did not feel particularly excited. It was very early in the morning and I was tired. However, it was a great relief to breathe fresh air again and to stretch the legs after the cramp of sitting in the boat. These minor considerations outweighed for the present any thought that we were free.

About half a mile up the hill, the major halted us. He said that he would go ahead and find someone to advise us where to go. In the meantime we should wait for him. We sat down, glad to have a rest, while he and one other disappeared into the darkness.

It was not long before they were back again. They were in a state of great excitement, talking below their breath in voluble Greek. There were exclamations from all around me and consternation prevailed. I soon discovered what it was all about. The major had met a shepherd and asked him where the nearest Turkish authorities were to be found. He had discovered to his horror that we were on Lemnos and not Imbros. We knew that Lemnos was heavily garrisoned with German troops and the shepherd said that the island was crowded with them. We had been lucky not to run into them. We were in grave danger.

I was too tired to be alarmed by this news. I was momentarily disappointed and then accepted the situation and found it entertaining. Our drunken skipper had put us once more into a precarious position. We hustled down the hill, my companions whispering excitedly about treachery and muttering the direst threats about what they would do to the captain.

We found the villain just preparing to sail. It was fortunate that he had found it necessary to have a little sleep before departing. A gesticulating group was quickly round him and described with a wealth of gesture what his future would be if we were caught. His squint became even more pronounced as he tried unavailingly to get in a word in self-defence.

The major cut the argument short and we climbed on board as quickly as possible. We cast off and the motor chugged at full speed. This time the major insisted on remaining on deck to make sure that no further mistakes were made. Already the first streaks of dawn were in the sky and we still had two or three hours' sailing ahead of us.

Fortunately, we were still favoured with a following breeze. We ran under sail with the engine at full speed. Our main concern was to reach the shores of Imbros before the air patrol came over. If the wind stayed favourable it was calculated that we would just do it. If we ran into a patrol boat it was just unfortunate; we still had to accept that risk.

With the major and one other up on deck it was decidedly easier below, but we were still cramped, and physical discomfort occupied most of our attention. It helped to keep the party from undue concern on any other score. We were very uncomfortable.

It seemed ages before we arrived. It had been daylight for some time. As we drew near the shore, at last the major allowed us to emerge on deck. We crowded up into the fresh air. Away behind us in the distance was Lemnos, the trap into which we had nearly fallen. To port, the jagged outline of Samothrace stuck out of the water like an inverted saw. The mountain ridges looked sharp as knives. Ahead of us lay Imbros. The wooded shores rose gently to the hills behind. We were approaching a long stretch of sandy beach.

The beach was steep and we ran close in before grounding. This time it was true. We were free at last. We had escaped from the Germans. Somehow it was an anticlimax. We had thought so much of this moment that when it came we found it commonplace. Physically, there was little change in our condition or environment. True, we were ashore. But we had been ashore on Lemnos, and in Greece for that matter. The difference was that this shore was free. We were no longer under the domination of the Germans. The difference was one of spirit, not of substance. It required the vision of the spirit to perceive and the sensitivity of the soul to feel. At eight o'clock in the morning, after a night of adventure, we had neither vision nor sensitivity. We just jumped ashore and walked up the beach.

We had not been ashore ten minutes before there was a familiar drone in the sky. Looking up, we saw a Junkers 88 passing low down out to sea. It was the patrol. Twenty minutes earlier it would have caught us and we should have gone down in a hail of bullets. Now it was just another aeroplane, flying aimlessly to an unknown destination.

V

Arrived safely on Turkish soil, the question was what to do next. There was no one in sight and no sign of habitation. We sat around on the grass; some said one thing and others another. Some were in favour of sending a representative to look for the nearest village. Others thought that we should disguise our point of arrival by walking round the coast first. There was general disagreement. I sat and listened.

Finally, I felt it was time to take charge and assumed responsibility for the whole party. I told them that we should go together to the nearest village. I would then speak to the Turkish gendarmerie with a view to getting in touch with our Embassy at Ankara as soon as possible. They accepted my authority and agreed to my plan. We walked steadily for an hour before there was any sign of habitation. Then we met some shepherds who told us that the village was just a little further on.

The village lay among orchards a little way back from the coast. It was a typical Greek village. The island of Imbros had been Greek up till 1923 when it was ceded to the Turks. Now it was Turkish-controlled and Greek-occupied.

We were met in the outskirts by a few of the local inhabitants who immediately engaged in rapid conversation with my companions. They were obviously delighted to see them and asked eagerly about their homeland. Soon there was quite a crowd round us. Two large Turkish military policemen appeared on the fringe of the crowd to find out what was going on.

I greeted them in Turkish, "Nasil sinis?" — How do you do? Memni spoke fluent Turkish and he acted as interpreter for me. I explained that we had escaped from the Germans and that I wished to communicate with the British Embassy in Ankara as quickly as possible. I mentioned that I was a personal friend of the Turkish chief of the air staff, whom I had known previously when I had been instructing the Turkish Air Force for six months in 1940.

General Sefik Cakmak's name obviously made an impression on the big, stolid policemen. They asked if I was in charge of the party as a whole, and I told them that I was. One of them then disappeared to telephone to his headquarters while the other stood by to take charge of us. We sat on the grass, surrounded by all the village.

It was not long before the policeman reappeared again. His orders were to take us to the military headquarters of Imbros in the middle of the island, some twenty kilometres away. There were no roads or vehicles, so we had to walk. We set off, headed by the policemen with their rifles slung over their shoulders. Our ragged party tailed along behind them. I marched in front with the major and Memni.

The country was very like Greece. Mountains rose on every side, and we marched along a rough trail through the wooded valleys. These were cultivated in small patches, and orchards and vineyards rose on the lower slopes of the hills on either side of us.

After about three hours we came to a big village and were escorted to the police-station there. Here we met a police officer and told our story to him again. While we were waiting there, a deputation from the village arrived to ask whether they might be permitted to feed us. The Turks agreed readily enough and we were allowed to go out into the village street.

We were immediately surrounded by a mob of excited Greek villagers. The ladies of the village spread a beautiful embroidered tablecloth on the street and people came from all quarters, bearing gifts. There was rich dark island honey and freshly cooked fish. There was a huge basinful of hot rice and another basinful of delicious fresh salad with oil and herbs;

there were also several chickens. Then there was white bread as well as brown, and butter and cheese. The table was soon crammed with food of every kind.

We did not have to be encouraged to eat. We were ravenously hungry and fell upon the delicacies without further ado. Never in my experience had I eaten such a delicious meal. Everything seemed to taste perfect. We crammed ourselves with food till we could eat no more. After ten months of starvation diet, this first meal was an experience we should never forget. We were full of gratitude for it and for the warmth and kindliness of the village folk who fussed around us to make us welcome.

Our Turkish policemen announced that it was time to leave. We set off once more. There was much ground to be covered before nightfall.

I was surprised at my stamina. It was something new. I noticed some of my friends lagging and weary while I felt fresh and ready for anything. We walked at a good pace. Just before dusk we came in sight of our destination, a large village nestling among green fields and orchards in a wide valley. We were taken straight to a large brick hall where bedding had been arranged for us and there was a hot meal of rice and bread and chicken waiting for us.

In the gathering darkness we stretched our tired limbs on the floor and ate. Immediately afterwards we sorted out our bedding and fell asleep. We were safe at last and we hardly noticed it.

XII

THE ROAD TO FREEDOM

I

Theoretically, I was now free to return home. By international law, the Turks were bound to repatriate me as soon as it was established that I was an escaped prisoner-of-war. It is only evaders and refugees who are liable to internment in a neutral country. Moreover, I had spent six months in Turkey earlier on in the war, teaching bombing and gunnery to the Turkish Air Force. I knew many of the leading figures in the country and had many friends, both among the Turks and in diplomatic circles. So I did not anticipate any trouble in getting from Turkey back to Egypt.

My expectations, however, proved to be a little optimistic. To the Turks at Imbros, I was a ragged stranger whose identity had to be established. Moreover, I had arrived with twenty Greek officers whose legal status was by no means clear. We were therefore kept in close confinement for some time. We spent four long days at Imbros, confined to the village hall, while the Turkish authorities waited for disposal intructions for us.

Then we were shipped from Imbros to the Dardanelles. At Cannakale we were taken under escort to a Turkish military hospital. We were confined in one of the wards there and were not permitted to leave the hospital premises. This was ostensibly a period of quarantine to make sure that we did not develop any peculiar diseases. Actually, it gave the Turkish authorities time to check up on our identity.

We all found this period of waiting very trying. We had

escaped from the Germans only to be put in prison by the Turks. The major and Memni and I even discussed plans for escape from the hospital.

The Turks fed us well. We were all thin from prolonged lack of food. So the two weeks of rest and eating went a long way to restoring our physical condition to normal. We put on weight rapidly.

The time at Çannakale was valuable also psychologically, as it acclimatised us gradually to the feeling of being back in civilisation again. We were not plunged straight into the so-called normal life of Cairo or London. It gave us time to adjust our attitude to the new conditions.

I used to sit in the sunshine on the shores of the Dardanelles within the hospital grounds and watch the ships pass up and down the historic straits. So much blood had been spilt here for freedom. I would muse on the strange truth that freedom is a state of mind more than a state of body. I began to realise how much I had been a prisoner to myself all through my life. I saw too how communities and nations are bound by the same invisible chains of selfish desire. I longed for complete freedom for myself, for my friends, for the world.

One day, as I sat in the sun, a Turkish doctor came up and sat with me. He was a very pleasant fellow and spoke good English. We chatted of my previous experiences in Turkey. I told him that I was very anxious to make contact with my old chief, the air attaché at the British embassy in Ankara, Air Vice Marshal R. A. George.

The doctor said that he knew the local British consul in Çannakale and that he would undertake to tell him that I was here. Two days later the consul appeared at the hospital, having been granted official permission to visit me. I told him about myself, giving full details of my escape, and asked him what could be done to rescue my friends whom I had had to leave behind. He promised to bring everything to the notice of the authorities concerned and assured me that they would be all right. His assurance greatly relieved my mind. It was evident from what he said that Bill and Harry and the others would be well provided for.

A few more days passed and then the commandant of the hospital sent for me to tell me that I was to be handed over to the British. I thanked him for his care of us in the hospital and quickly prepared to leave. It was a wrench saying good-bye to my Greek friends. They had done so much for me. I promised the major and Memni that I would do my best to see that they were sent to join the Greek Army in Egypt. That was all I could do. The others crowded round me and we said good-bye affectionately. We had been through memorable days together.

I was handed over to the British consul by a Turkish officer. He demanded a receipt for me. We laughed and the consul wrote out a slip of paper: "Received from the Turkish Government one Squadron Leader Edward Howell." He signed and dated it and handed it over. I had made another step to freedom.

One evening, a few days later, I boarded the passenger ship which runs from Istanbul to Izmir. I had a cabin to myself and slept soundly. Travelling on the boat with me, I found two old friends from the French colony at Izmir — the Girauds. They were astounded to see me. They had heard that I had been killed in Crete. Then news had come through that I was wounded and a prisoner. Although I had never received them, my friends in Izmir had contributed to send me parcels of food and clothes through the Red Cross. It was my first contact with the old world I had lived in before. It was strange and delightful to move among old friends again.

Also travelling on the ship, and eating at a nearby table, were two civilians who were obviously German officers. One was a typical German colonel with a bald head, thick neck and wearing a monocle. He was accompanied by a younger man who had lost his left arm. I was amused at the situation. I was dressed in rags and had just escaped from a German prison-camp and here I was sitting in the first-class dining saloon at the next table to them. They had no idea who I was or where I had come from, but they were soon to learn.

We turned the corner into the lovely sea loch which leads up to Smyrna. Called Izmir by the Turks since 1923, when they took it over from the Greeks, the town stands in beautiful surroundings. From the water front, it rises up in terraces on the face of the steep hillside. To the east the loch continues for a time and then ends at the abrupt barrier of the Manissa Mountains, rising sheer up to 6,000 feet. It was a familiar sight to me, as this was where I had spent six months in 1940. In the distance, I could pick out the Izmir Palas Hotel where I had stayed. Memories came crowding back.

We tied up alongside the jetty. Among the crowd waiting to meet the boat, I saw the tall figure of an old friend — Billy Hughes. He had been sent by the British Consul General to meet me. Near him I noticed the German consul, an arrogant young Nazi who had taken great pains to try to discover all about me when I had been there before. I knew him by sight and realised that he would know that I had been a prisoner of war. I looked forward to seeing his face as I walked off the ship.

I came down the gangway just ahead of the German colonel and his companion. The consul's face was a study as he saw me. His polite smile of greeting for his compatriots froze into a look of astonishment and dismay.

Billy Hughes was the same as ever. He gave me a great welcome and shepherded me through the crowds to a waiting car. I was to stay at his flat. We had been good friends during my previous stay there and it was a joy to be with him again. I asked for all my other friends and caught up quickly on the news of the community. Billy asked no questions. He was concerned with my comfort. As soon as we got to the flat I had a bath and dressed in one of his suits. It hung loosely round me but was at least respectable.

Later that night we went out together with another old friend and sat in the open-air restaurant, admiring the reflections in the water. We had a delicious dinner and I told them what had happened to me. As we sat there, other friends came up to greet me. It was a foretaste of the welcome home which I had looked forward to for so long.

The next day I hurried round to the Consulate to confirm that arrangements were in hand for the rescue of my friends in Greece and the release of the officers at Cannakale. Later, I went visiting all my old friends. They were enchanted with my dramatic appearance and safe arrival. I wanted to stay on for some time to be with them. But the embassy had instructed that I should get to Ankara as soon as possible. So Billy put me on a train that night. As we stood on the platform saying good-bye to each other, I noticed the German colonel and his companion again. They were being seen off by their consul. They looked across at me in obvious consternation. Billy and I laughed heartily.

Just eight hours later, at seven o'clock, the train pulled into the station at Eskisehir. This town lies in the middle of the Sakarya Plain some 3,000 feet above sea-level and halfway to Ankara from Izmir. It was the chief training centre for the Turkish Air Force and I had spent some time there during my previous stay in Turkey. I looked out of the carriage window at the familiar railway station. To my astonishment, I saw a group of Turkish Air Force officers with their wives, scanning the train eagerly. They were old friends, warned by Billy Hughes that I would be passing.

I jumped out and greeted them. They were delighted to see me and had brought little presents with them. Stout, smiling Jemal was there with his charming wife. He had been a faithful friend and interpreter. Then there was "Chorlu Charlie" Hikmet — a cheerful rascal who had been my own interpreter and with whom I had taken part in many escapades. There were others too. It was a wonderful welcome.

We stood on the platform, exchanging news, until the train was ready to pull out again. As we left, I went into the restaurant car to have breakfast. Seated at the table on the other side of the corridor were the two Germans. I was amused to see them look pointedly away out of the window as I sat down. The Turkish waiter bustled up and took my order.

About half an hour out from Eskisehir, there was a sudden roar as an aircraft flashed past within inches of the roof of the train. I looked out and saw it pull up into a steep climbing turn. Then there was another roar as a second aircraft followed it, and another. It was my friends from Eskisehir. They had hurried back from the station to their aeroplanes and were waving me farewell in characteristic Air Force fashion. At that point, the railway line ran across flat grassland without a tree or obstacle of any kind. This meant that my friends could fly with their propeller tips clipping the grass. They came straight at the train, pulling up at the very last moment to clear it by a fraction. It was fun. I hastened to an open window and waved to them as they came at me.

When I got back to my seat, I noticed that the Germans were very preoccupied with their plates. This had been too much for them. I could not help laughing at the dramatic turn of events. One day a hunted man, the next welcomed by everybody in the presence of my hunters. The situation gave me great satisfaction and I noticed my Turkish waiter was also relishing the occasion.

At Ankara I was met by one of the secretaries from the Embassy. He took me to my hotel and explained that the air attaché was waiting to see me.

I found my late chief, Air Vice Marshal Bobby George, in his usual cheerful spirits. He gave me a great welcome. Then I had dinner with the Ambassador — Sir Hugh Knatchbull-Hugheson — and told him my story. My few days at Ankara were crowded with welcome lunches and dinners from old friends.

My first task was to go to visit the Greek ambassador. I told him about all my friends whom I had had to leave behind, both at Çannakale and also in Greece. He had already heard about Major Constas and the others and assured me that arrangements were being made for them to be transferred to Egypt.

He also promised to see what could be done to look after the others.

Although I was very grateful for all the expressions of friendship and the warmth of my welcome everywhere, I was inwardly becoming a little disturbed. Everywhere I went people congratulated me on my escape. They did not understand. How could they? I felt baffled to explain to them that I had had so little to do with the success of my venture. I felt like a man who had been to a distant planet and then is faced with the task of describing it to people who had never been there. The two states of life were so utterly different.

After a few days at Ankara I flew back to Egypt. A Turkish airliner took me across the Taurus Mountains to Adana. From there I went on by an Egyptian airliner. We landed at Cyprus and in Palestine. The airfields at Nicosia and Lydda were familiar spots to me. I had been there many times in the past. But landing at Lydda this time had a new significance. Stepping out of the plane, I set foot on the Holy Land. The dusty airfield was more than a halting place en route for Cairo. It was the end of one pilgrimage and the beginning of another. I had finally escaped from the enemy. Now, in the familiar surroundings of my old haunts and among the familiar company of my own folk and friends, I was starting a further stage on the road to freedom.

III

Back in Cairo I had much to do. I had a room at Shepheard's Hotel. At the first opportunity, I hurried to my old tailor's nearby to get myself a uniform to wear. Then I reported to the headquarters of the Royal Air Force in the Middle East. It was exciting to walk in at the familiar entrance and go up the lift I had used so often when I had worked there myself. I went to the office of an old friend, Air Commodore Lee. I knocked on the door and walked in. He was sitting at his desk. He looked up automatically and said, "Yes?" in an inquiring tone. I watched his face change; it took some time. Recognition and amazement were simultaneous. He leapt to his feet as if he had seen a ghost. I sat down and told him my story.

Almost my first task in Cairo was to check up on what arrangements had been made for my friends back in Greece. To my great joy and surprise I found that they had already reached Palestine. Harry Brown and Stuart and Bill, together with a number of our Greek friends, had been picked up by a smuggler's boat at Ayo Nikolaos and had reached safety. Stuart and Bill were to be shipped straight back home to Australia. Harry elected to rejoin his unit in Egypt. They were later decorated for their gallantry.

I had a happy time going round Cairo, making people think they were seeing ghosts. Several of my friends, on seeing me for the first time, hastily vowed to abstain from alcohol. It was entertaining. I arranged a dinner party to celebrate the occasion. We had a large table in the garden at Shepheard's. We dined and danced and rejoiced to be together again. The number of the table was thirty-three — my old squadron. I thought of the host of friends who were absent, yet present, the gallant company who had given everything.

There were other parties too, given in my honour. I tried to recapture the careless irresponsibility of days that were past and gone. Then, adventure had been to behave outrageously, to get drunk, to flirt and be foolish. Now, all that seemed empty and childish. I had tasted real adventure and the flavour of the old was sour.

As soon as I was able, I got in touch with Madame Jacquier, the wife of my French friend who had nursed me so faithfully during my first weeks in hospital. I was able to deliver his messages and was delighted to hear that he was safe and well, although a prisoner in Germany. I had feared that he would be shot. I also wrote to the relatives of various of my friends, like the parents of Dick Mann and Butch, to give them first-hand news of their safety.

Among others whom I met in Cairo was Sandy Thomas. I

had not seen him since his daring attempt to escape from the hospital at Athens. Now I met him swimming in the pool at the Gezira Club. He was surprised and delighted to see me. We chatted of old days. Sandy had succeeded in escaping from the prison-camp at Salonika. He had had many adventures in the mountains and it had taken him six months to reach Egypt. His initiative and resource and personal courage had been unfailing all through. He had worked hard to earn his freedom. Now he elected to rejoin his regiment, where he was later to achieve distinction through his daring and leadership. Together we visited various Greek communities in Cairo, to express our appreciation of all that their countrymen had done for us.

My first Sunday in Cairo, I went eagerly to the little Scots church of St. Andrew. My father had been there for a year while I was at school. But although I had spent many months in Cairo previously, this was my first visit to it. The church was full of troops. They were mostly New Zealanders and a New Zealand padre was in the pulpit. The simple Scots service moved me deeply. In some way it completed the link between the precious days of childhood and those through which I had just passed. In that service, an experience begun as a child and taken up again as a prisoner, became integrated. The old psalms kindled the memory. The words were amazingly appropriate:

"O give thanks unto the Lord, for He is good: for His mercy endureth for ever. Let the redeemed of the Lord say so, whom He hath redeemed from the hand of the enemy; and gathered them out of the lands, from the East, and from the West, from the North, and from the South. They wandered in the wilderness in a solitary way; they found no city to dwell in. Hungry and thirsty, their soul fainted in them. Then they cried unto the Lord in their trouble, and He delivered them out of their distresses. He brought them out of darkness and the shadow of death and brake their bonds asunder."

203

I stayed on for Holy Communion, and left the church light of heart and filled with gratitude.

I reported myself back on duty. I was taken to see Air Chief Marshal Sir Arthur Tedder. He asked me to lunch with him at his home and I told him my story. Behind his informal manner lay one of the most clear-sighted minds in Britain. Tedder's unfailing judgment of men and situations, allied with brilliant staff work and great personal charm, had already made him an outstanding Commander-in-Chief. He was destined to be at the vital centre of the great Anglo-American team which was later to advance in triumph to Berlin. Tedder told me to put in a report in writing for record purposes. I occupied myself with this for a few days. He also authorised my immediate return to England by air.

I had already cabled home from Ankara to announce my safe arrival. An almost incoherent reply had come from my father and mother. They could not understand how it came about that I was now in Cairo. The last they had heard from me was through the Red Cross from the hospital in Salonika. They had pictured me in some distant prison hospital in Germany, crippled and confined. Instead, here I was, cabling cheerfully from Cairo.

But in some strange way, while I had been escaping, my mother had sensed what was happening to me. Now the faint whispers of intuition were reinforced. She was certain I had escaped. My father, always the realist in the family, doubted it. He assumed that I must have been repatriated by the Germans and pictured me lying in some hospital in Egypt. Instead, I lay in comparative luxury in Shepheard's Hotel, rapidly putting on weight again, and spending the afternoons in the swimming pool at the Gezira Club.

Rommel and his Afrika Corps started to advance rapidly towards Alexandria. It was the end of June 1942. As the reports came in that the Germans had retaken Mersa Matruh, I began to wonder where the advance would stop. People in Egypt became more than a little apprehensive. There was consider-

able evacuation of civilians to the south and emergency preparations for local defence were instituted. A party of Egyptian
students marched across the Bulak Bridge with banners, "We
want Rommel." The situation was tense. The enemy was ham-
mering at our gates.

I began to wonder whether I should stay in the Middle East
to help. It looked as though I was running away to go home at
this point. Instinctively, I feared public opinion. But there was
little I could do in my present crippled state. I could not fly.
I had volunteered to go back into Greece again to liaise with
the resistance forces, but I was not really suitable for that either
with my impaired health and lack of knowledge of Greek.

I prayed to be shown what to do and not to be influenced by
fear of opinion on the one hand or personal desire on the other.
The conviction grew that God had a purpose for me in going
home. It was part of a greater plan. He would see that I served
to the best advantage. It was the next step on the road to freedom. Reassured I went ahead with preparations to leave on the
first available plane. My fears proved groundless. The enemy
was halted in the desert and the name of the place was El
Alamein. A new general arrived to take command of the Desert
Army. His name was Montgomery. The tide was about to turn.

IV

I was coming home. The sunlight dazzled as it reflected from
the unbroken layer of cloud below. The Liberator roared on.
For me, the aircraft was appropriately named. We had been
travelling for hours without sighting land and the cloud stretched
unendingly ahead. Suddenly I noticed two specks in the distance.
They grew rapidly larger, fighters coming to intercept us.
Unerringly, they went into position up-sun and came in on a
perfect quarter attack. But we were recognised and this was a
greeting, not an encounter. They were making sure that English
skies remained inviolate. Flashing past us, they were soon out of
sight again.

I strained to find a gap in the curtain below. It started to thin in places, like the worn patches on an old coat. There were occasional glimpses of the sea below as if through lace. Then holes appeared through which the white caps could be seen clearly thousands of feet below. Thinner still, and we could distinguish the patches of sunlight on the water like the colour on a quilt. The cloud thinned until it became broken, huge masses of cumulus like icebergs, drifting majestically to a far destination.

Then, quite suddenly, we were crossing the coastline. I saw the cliffs and coves of England, dappled in sunlight. It threw into sharp relief of colour and shade the green of little fields, the dark patches of the woods, the huddled villages of thatch and stream by ancient church and stately manor. After two years abroad, it was breathtaking in its beauty, stirring in its familiarity, and almost painfully precious. In that moment I saw what we were fighting for and sensed the inspiration which could make understandable all the sacrifices of war.

I gazed intent at the scene below. Soon we were flying over familiar country. Landmarks went by like a procession of ghosts. They recalled happy memories of old friends, so many of whom had given their lives that all this might be preserved. I thought of the fantastic cost of our heritage in the lives spent in its creation.

Soon we were circling an airfield in a wide sweep. The motors changed their tune. The aircraft shuddered as the wheels and flaps were lowered. We touched down lightly, rolled smoothly to the end of the runway, and turned off to the perimeter track. The motors coughed and spluttered and were still. I was in England.

A few greetings, a word of thanks to the crew, and I walked away into the sweet scent of the summer evening. Here, there was no stench or dust or flies, but quiet lanes rich with the perfume of mown hay and hawthorn hedges. I thought again of the vision I had seen. How was it that England had come to mean so much to so many?

I thought of the things we loved about Britain, her traditions of liberty and courage, of justice, faith and honesty; clearly they were far from perfect, but they were extremely precious to us. We were proud of our country's achievements over the centuries, in war and peace. We loved the way of life handed on to us by those who had worked and fought to establish it. Chiefly, I suppose, we loved our homes and families and friends, as people do in every country. To us, their welfare and safety, the maintenance of their cherished place in our lives and in the life of our country was paramount. For this we had no hesitation in sacrificing what was needed, even to our lives if required.

During the war many lived sacrificially, giving much and ready to give all. We did this because we believed it was necessary if we were to save our country from being taken over by enemy forces and enemy ideas, alien to our traditions. We did not think too much about what our national philosophy really meant, to us or to others. We had an obvious and powerful enemy to face and defeat. That was enough. Or was it?

We knew what we were fighting against much more than what we were fighting for. We thought the future could be left to itself. Someone else should maintain the intangible structure and values of national life, and change them too where necessary. The politicians and parsons, the educators and writers should look after these things. It was their business; we would do our duty, let them do theirs. This kind of abandonment of that common responsibility for our democratic life and institutions would be at the root of many of the problems our nation was to face in the years that lay ahead. Post-war Britain would be very different from pre-war Britain. If we did not take responsibility for how it changed we could not blame others for changes we did not approve.

In that summer of 1942, however, these problems seemed remote. We still seemed to be in danger of losing the war. Three long years of sweat and blood and tears lay ahead of us. On reporting back to the Air Ministry I was immediately granted some leave. I headed for home.

The train puffed along the little line running from Leuchars to St. Andrews. My heart was very full as I gazed at the familiar scenes. There was the spot on the estuary where I had shot my first duck in the cold December dawn. There were the sands where we used to ride, and the famous links where the game of golf began. The lovely silhouette of St. Andrews came into view, with its clean grey buildings, the sweep of sands, and the grandeur of great rocks jutting into the North Sea. Above them all, the University Chapel tower kept watch over the centuries and pointed to the stars.

My father waited for me on the platform. He had aged a good deal and was frail for all his height. He was thin and a little bent. But his face lit as he saw me and he straightened, shaking off the years. He had on his familiar old grey suit and soft hat. My heart leapt to him as we stood silent holding hands. In that instant, the years rolled away and I was a little child again, holding his father's hand. There was so much I owed to him and so much to say. We were silent still, and the current flowed between us in the silent harmony of complete understanding.

We walked through the historic old streets, not saying much, and down a familiar little alley. There was the old house which had seen three centuries of history go by. Never in the ebb and flow of life around its walls had there been a more satisfying reunion. My mother met me at the door; she had been afraid to come to the station. We held each other close and our hearts overflowed. I had come home.

XIII

"PER ARDUA AD ASTRA"*

I

Home was the end of one adventure and the beginning of others. I had completed the first stage of my escape to live. The road to new freedom and new life led on into the distance. I had come, through difficulties, some little way along it. The stars were still distant. Full freedom was still a far-off goal and many more adventures in faith lay ahead.

After some leave at home in that memorable summer I reported to hospital, where the surgeons made a wonderful job of mending my crippled arms. It was at the R.A.F. Convalescent Hospital at Torquay that I met my brother David again. He had volunteered for the Royal Air Force as aircrew and had been trained as a navigator in the United States. Now he was back in England completing his training before going on operations in Bomber Command. He came to visit me one weekend.

It was a great event meeting him again. I owed him so much for the part he had played in helping to show me the way, and I had so much to tell him about it all. We walked together through the quiet Devonshire lanes and I told him about the things I had experienced. Naturally he was delighted and told me how he and his friends had been praying regularly for me, as had my father and mother. I am sure these prayers played their part.

I was interested to see how David regarded the supernatural and the miraculous in my escape as somehow natural and

* "Through difficulties to the Stars", Motto of the Royal Air Force.

209

normal. Miracles are, after all, a natural and normal part of the realm of the Spirit. He was more interested in what I was planning to be and do now. The past is there to build on, not to live in. My experiences had been given me to use, not to sit on. He wanted to know how I was going to use them to the best effect.

This meeting turned out to be a further milestone for me. I began to look ahead to what was wanted of me now and realised how much I had to learn. David's disciplined life, his getting up in the morning, no matter how early, so as to spend an unhurried hour seeking God's guidance; his emphasis on absolute not relative moral standards; his preoccupation with other people's needs and how to help them; his aim to stop at nothing short of a world remade under God's rule; all these things made a deep and lasting impression on me. My own discipline had been slack, my standards low, my interests petty by comparison. I determined to be different in future.

Another point he made that day was that I should be sure that I was starting off my new life with a clean slate. I should do everything I could to put right the past. This same thought had already occurred to me, but I had been avoiding it. Now, I went ahead with a difficult programme of righting some of the things I had done wrong in the past, involving restitution, repayments and apologies where these were long overdue but still possible. It was clearly right to do this however hurtful to my pride and pocket. It was a load off my mind to feel bound by no debts or shackles with the past.

David also helped me to understand something further. Up to now I had walked along the road to freedom on my own. I had been more or less alone in my venture. From now on, I realised, I was one of an army marching together under God's orders. It was normal to work together. Without the help of friends I should make many unnecessary mistakes and accomplish far less. "God normally provides people around you," he said, "with whom you are meant to become close friends. You need them and they need you. Together you can do much."

From then on he helped me to get in touch with people in Moral Re-Armament, which was to play a big part in my future.

Shortly after this meeting I was still at the Convalescent Hospital at Torquay. One Sunday morning I woke as usual and spent an hour in devotion, Bible study, prayer and meditation. I asked God what He wanted me to do that day, a normal question to which I expected a normal reply. In my own mind I saw myself spending the morning writing some important letters in my room.

Instead, a persistent thought came that I should go to church. Of course it was Sunday, but I resisted it with all the arguments I could muster for writing the letters instead. To me they seemed urgent and I would not get them done later. Church would be just another formality. I knew no one there. Yet every time I prayed again "not my will but Thine be done", and meant it, I had the same thought: "Go to Church at eleven o'clock"! Eventually I accepted, still reluctantly, that this might be God's guidance and that I should obey. I got ready and left my room on the third floor of the building and walked a quarter of a mile up the road to the nearby church.

I was just entering the door as the clock struck eleven. At that moment there was a sudden roar overhead. Two enemy fighters flashed past. Anti-aircraft guns opened up at them as they turned and sped back out to sea. Each had dropped two large bombs into the basement of the hospital. After a ten-second delay these exploded and a large part of the building was destroyed.

I hurried back to see what I could do to help. Many others were already at work trying to get people out from the debris. With my crippled arms there was not much I could do, so I went back to church and prayed. Later, I climbed a shaky fire escape to the third floor to my room. I found my bed, on which I would have been seated doing my letters. The room was a shambles. One wall was open to seaward and my mattress was slashed through in strips from end to end by flying glass.

In the next room another convalescent officer had been in

211

his bed. His head was found on the lawn a hundred yards away. We had lost a good many killed and many more wounded. Once more the still small voice of God, only just trusted and obeyed, had saved me. I was overwhelmed with gratitude and wonder. My Bible and a number of papers and other valuables were safe in a drawer and I lost nothing of real value.

As the war went on, God's guidance became more and more something on which I felt I could rely, not necessarily to save my life, but to lead me to be and do what was right for me personally as well as for God's wider purposes. David experienced this too all through his tour of operations on Stirling Bombers where the casualty rates were appalling. His crew and one other were the only survivors of those with whom they had started their tour.

David won the Distinguished Flying Cross for gallantry and a commission as officer as well. On his second tour, on Lancasters, the aircraft was destroyed over the Ruhr. The whole crew was able to bale out and descend safely by parachute, to be captured and spend the remaining months of the war as prisoners. All of them came out of it safely in the end. David's experience of God's guidance and providence, and the adequacy of the Holy Spirit for him at all times, was similar to mine. "My grace is sufficient for you." Many of our friends found the same. Those who died in action would also know their sacrifice was a part of the same pattern. "All things work together for good to those who love God."

II

Towards the end of that year I was passed fit for work again. I was thrilled to find that I could once more fly an aeroplane. After a little practice, getting used to the limitations in strength and movement of my arms, I found myself able to reach and operate all controls, at least on single-engined aircraft.

I persuaded the doctors to allow me a normal flying category and flew myself about until the end of the war. I had hoped to go back on operations again, but by this time I had been posted to the Air Ministry for duty on the Air Staff. Since I had been an armament specialist before the war, I now became concerned with the operational requirements for new weapons for the whole of the Air Force. It was a big job and I was kept busy at it for the next two years.

During this time, I was appointed chairman of a joint Anglo-American Weapons Committee and took part in the Allied planning for D Day. After the invasion I was sent on various missions into France, Belgium, Holland and Germany, and also into Norway to report on the sunken German battleship *Tirpitz* in Tromsö Fjord. After the end of the war in Europe I was posted to Washington to serve on the British Joint Staff Mission and also on the Joint Target Group with the United States Air Force at the Pentagon.

This period of over two years working on the staff in wartime gave me the chance to relate what I had learned to my new circumstances. I discovered that my new way of living was just as helpful in the daily problems I now faced as it had been during my escape. My commitment remained to learn to know and love God better, to ask Him to guide me daily, and to be prepared to trust and obey Him regardless. I had to continue to search for what seemed morally right and to try to follow my highest convictions in faith.

Working on the Air Staff in fact was no different from working anywhere else. Basically, there were many things to be done. They had to be done as right as possible. There were many people with whom I had to work, both above and below me. Relations with them were to be made and kept as right as possible.

Pride and self-will, jealousy and ambition, envy and anger, fear and greed are the common saboteurs in any job, liable to damage teamwork and efficiency in any working group. When things went wrong, as they did from time to time, some at least of the blame was in me. A change of heart, with honest apologies where these were due, was often enough to renew broken links.

Sometimes, too, God revealed other ways of helping to restore good relations where these were damaged.

There were larger issues too. How to help to create good teamwork between the Air Ministry and the Commands at home and abroad? How to help to build inter-Service and inter-Allied unity? I frequently found myself in a position to play some part, great or small, in affecting these major issues as well. When I asked God to show me ways in which to be useful, there usually seemed to be something I could do.

On the 15th of August, 1945, the war ended with victory in the Far East. By then I was home again in St. Andrews awaiting posting.

I sat at the desk in my father's study listening to the victory bells pealing from the Town Kirk steeple. They sounded the national anthems and then some of the old Scots tunes. "Even as a bird, out of the fowler's snare, escapes away, so is our soul set free." I was deeply moved and thankful. This was the historic day of victory for which so many had given their lives.

I could hear my mother busy about the house with many a loving touch. It had been raining and the air was fresh with the scent of roses. The old town was peaceful, rejoicing quietly in victory, brooding over the centuries.

My father seemed very close as I gazed out of the window at the garden, bright with flowers. Earlier, my mother and I had visited his grave together. It was nearly two years old now. We had stood there quietly, looking out from the ruins of the ancient cathedral over the sweep of the east sands and beyond to the rugged line of cliffs. The gulls were soaring on the sea wind, crying over the old tombs like liberated spirits who fain would leave some word behind.

I sat still and remembered many comrades who had sacrificed their lives for this moment. Out of the twenty of us at the Royal Air Force College at Cranwell in the University Entry of 1935, only one other remained. There were scores of others too whom I remembered, many of my closest friends. I could not believe that they were not around somewhere, an unseen host in the

214

realm of the spirit, now free as the air in which they fought. Somehow we were still flying in formation. We should land at the same destination.

The war of arms had ended. Millions of fighting men would be returning home with one task completed. How many would enlist again for the struggle which lay ahead? On V Day our King had called upon us all to "restore the shattered fabric of civilisation". Who would respond to this call and aim to make our way of life so effective and attractive that it would draw the nations together in unity and strength? Someone had once said, "I, if I be lifted up, will draw all men unto Me". What could we do to play our part in realising this promise to unite humanity?

The old clock above the desk ticked away the hours as I sat, deep in thought and in prayer. Conviction grew. I had been shown the way. Now was the time to give all I could to it. Although I did not know it then, I was soon to be given the opportunity I needed.

After the war I was selected to go to the Staff College. On graduating from there I had my first post-war Medical Board. The doctors told me that the injuries to my arms meant the end of my flying career. After fourteen happy years in the Royal Air Force the time had come to close that chapter of my life. I was to be invalided from active service to the retired list.

I was sad, but also glad. The road to further freedom lay ahead. It would be as full of joy and of adventure as it had been before. The same star was still there to guide me and the same power to help me. The way to the stars was still the goal.

POSTSCRIPT

As demand for this book continues more than thirty years after the first edition, this new one is published with minor changes to bring it up to date. People constantly ask me: "Does it still work?" They want to know whether my experience of guidance and grace and miracles has carried on in later life.

The answer is that it has not only continued but also multiplied. For many years I worked, as my brother still does, as a full-time volunteer with the force of Moral Re-Armament across the world aiming to bring an answer to personal, national and international problems everywhere. Like a host of others, whose beginnings may have been less dramatic but none the less valid than my own, I have found that Frank Buchman's teaching, "When man listens, God speaks; when man obeys, God acts; when men change, nations change" is basic truth. It has been proved over and over again by those who apply it wholeheartedly.

In the course of this work we revisited Greece shortly after the war and traced as many as possible of those who had helped me in my escape. We were able to help some of their children to be educated at the Farm School near Salonika where my old friends of Dulag 183, Charles and Ann House, had returned to continue their vital work, more than ever necessary in post-war Greece. Recently my wife and I went to help there ourselves and renewed precious links with old friends in Greece. In such ways, and many others, the past plays its destined part in reshaping the future.

In the prevailing revival of concern everywhere for the reality of spiritual experience and moral change, perhaps this new edition can point the way for others to "Escape to Live" and join the multitudes who know what it is to be liberated and healed and put to work for God in the life of their nations.

ON FREEDOM

Who will not fight for freedom, dies a slave;
Who will not dare to live is doomed to death;
He lives indeed for ever on whose grave
Is writ: "He fought and dared with every breath."

Who will not give his all, will lose his way
And flounder on through life's brief passing hour
Aimless, by dreams and wishes led astray,
By hope of gain which, being won, turns sour.

Who'll fight and dare to live, shall yet be free
And, free, help liberate a world in chains;
Who'll give, and keep on giving all, shall see
The morning sun break through behind the rains.

He'll live in growing freedom all his days
And sing, with hosts of warriors, God's praise.

E.A.H.